"When my daughters, who were then nine and ten years old, and I first arrived in Los Angeles, we set about looking for 'our' church. Alone as we felt at that time, we hoped to find a preacher who would make us feel less so. Sure enough, the first day we walked into All Saints' Church and saw Greg Richards in the pulpit, I could picture him in my kitchen having coffee if something bad happened. It turned out just that way.

"This book is a great gift to those who have experienced grief or who are close to someone who has. It is written by a man of utter sincerity, practical wisdom, personal courage, and deep understanding. The book speaks as he does, with profound humanity and love."

Dixie Carter, actress and entertainer,
star of "Designing Woman" (CBS)

"*When Someone You Know Is Hurting* has been invaluable in helping me better understand family life crises."

Norma Freeman, MFCC; marriage and family
therapist and director of the Family Support
Center of Stephen S. Wise Temple, Los Angeles

"Greg Richards's beautiful book is a beacon for all of us in those difficult times when we need to truly 'be there' for someone. It is an invaluable resource which has helped me personally and professionally, and one which I will unhesitatingly recommend for my patients' reading."

Stephen A. Shoop, M.D., surgeon
Los Angeles

D0173819

"A must-read for all those who search for caring, compassionate, and sensitive words and acts to comfort the grieving."

The Honorable Robert K. Tanenbaum,
government official, attorney, and author

"The chapter dealing with hospital visitation should prove most helpful to anyone who is the least bit anxious about visiting in a medical institution. The material covers the important areas of concern and is presented in a 'pastoral' way which treats the reader gently and compassionately—thereby eliciting like behavior at the time of a visit. All in all, the many helpful suggestions here will enable one to make caring and meaningful hospital visits."

The Reverend David C. Walker,
chaplain and director of pastoral care,
the Hospital of the Good Samaritan,
Los Angeles

"Greg Richards has written a remarkable book that is filled with warmth and wisdom. This sensitive guide will become a constant companion to those who must comfort family and friends at the truly difficult times in life. It will remain in print for many years."

Albert D. Wheelon, Ph.D., physicist and author,
former chairman and C.E.O., Hughes Aircraft
Company

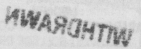

# WHEN SOMEONE YOU KNOW IS HURTING

## What You Can Do to Help

## M. Gregory Richards

Zondervan Publishing House
*Grand Rapids, Michigan*

HarperPaperbacks
*New York, New York*

*Divisions of HarperCollinsPublishers*

*When Someone You Know Is Hurting*
Copyright © 1994 by M. Gregory Richards
All rights reserved

Requests for information should be directed to:
Zondervan Publishing House
Grand Rapids, Michigan 49530

ISBN 0-06-104305-2

*Edited by Lori J. Walburg and J. Cheri McLaughlin*
*Cover design by Jeff Sharpton, Paz Design Group*

*Printed in the United States of America*

94  95  96  97  98 / OP / 5  4  3  2

*For those who have cared so much for me*
*Debbie, my bride*
*Vera and Mike, my parents*

# Contents

# Acknowledgments

This book would not have been possible without the patience and forbearance of my family. My wife, Debbie, has deciphered and criticized every word and encouraged me to persevere. My young sons, Michael and Matthew, have allowed me to carve hours out of virtually every holiday and family vacation for several years to complete this project. Their godfather, Jeffrey Sherwood, has been in on this since the first rough outline and has helped not only by words but by sharing in our times of crisis and loss and allowing us to share in his.

So many mentors have contributed to what I know about caring: the pastors of my youth, particularly the Reverend John K. Saville and the Reverend Harry R. Edwall; teachers in seminary and supervisors in field-work experiences; friends, parishioners, and colleagues who have trusted me to teach or counsel with them. I am especially grateful to the congregations I've served: St. Stephen's Episcopal Church in Whittier, California, and All Saints' Church in Beverly Hills, California. Students and faculty at Campbell Hall in North Hollywood, California, now allow me to share in their daily lives, for which I thank them and, especially, the Reverend Thomas G. Clarke, Headmaster.

Author friends have encouraged me (often with a kick) to get the job done. Robert K. Tanenbaum believed I had this book in me and shared from his celebrated writing talent; without him, there would be no book. Michael Cart waded through the manuscript with his gifts as an author and literary reviewer. The Reverend Terrance Sweeney and Pamela Shoop Sweeney, currently celebrating the publication of their two books, not only reviewed my manuscript but also helped promote it with publishers, constantly offering me optimistic support.

Lisa Brand Agnew and the Reverend David C. Walker, former church colleagues in Beverly Hills, made the manuscript presentable. Matthew Gandel prepared the final draft. Literary agent Michael Hamilburg, supported by his assistant Joan Socola, presented the manuscript to Zondervan Publishing House. Sandra Vander Zicht, acquisitions editor, shepherded the proposal through Zondervan, then to Harper Paperbacks, who copublished this book. Lori Walburg, associate editor, reviewed and edited the manuscript.

Many other friends helped me stay with this project with love, expertise, and patient support through the years. In no particular order, I thank Norma Freeman, Stephen Getzoff, Mary Wickes, John Tucker, Paul Schreibman, Louisa Jones, Dr. Albert Wheelon, Dr. Stephen Shoop, Robert Engols, The Reverend G. Bradford Hall, Edna Davidson, Michael Kazanjian, Laura and Lee Holdridge, Dr. Richard Herzberg, Dolly Wageman, Nancy Fuller, Suzanne Wickham, Dr. Alan Loy McGinnis, Lori Jones, Susanne Wilson, Ann Blewitt, Russell Chandler, Dixie Carter, Peb Jackson,

Michael Sumja, the Reverend Daniel Heischman, the Right Reverend Frederick H. Borsch, Rosalinda O'Neill, Richard Messer, William C. McMorran, Dr. Sanford M. Shapero, and my brothers in the Friars clergy group.

For these and many others, thanks be to God!

# Introduction

One beautiful spring day a young teenage boy sat trapped in a nearly empty school library. He was supposed to be researching for a term paper, but his heart—and his hormones—kept interfering. Then he made a discovery. In the shadows of a corner of the library, he found a lone book resting on a bottom shelf. Picking it up, his eyes widened as he read the title: *How to Hug.*

The boy hadn't realized that his school library carried books like this! Quickly, he placed it in the middle of a stack of books and walked as nonchalantly as possible to the checkout desk. As soon as the librarian had finished checking out the books, he gathered them up and left the library, walking as fast as he could. Back home, he shut himself in his room to carry out some exciting research. He pulled out the book *How to Hug.* He opened it. To his dismay, he found out that *How to Hug* was nothing other than volume seven of the encyclopedia!

This is a "how to" book—perhaps even a "how to hug" book—but it's also much more. Its scope has grown since my original purpose: to answer the daily questions of parishioners and acquaintances about what to do for and what to say to someone who is facing crisis or loss. I now look at caring for others in a more general way. Although this book focuses on crisis times, it also covers the caring that keeps our relationships alive, in good times and bad.

My own journey to become a loving, caring person took an extraordinary turn in the midst of a truly bad time.

\* \* \*

"I can't face those people. Their hurt is too great. I don't know what to say. I don't know what to do."

I was frightened out of my mind.

An eight-year-old boy had died tragically, suddenly, violently. On an outing with his parents and teenage sister, he fell off a cliff. Even worse, his older sister had made a heroic lunge, grasped the youngster's hands but a second too late, and watched him fall.

I had heard the radio report of a child falling off a mountain above Los Angeles. Neither the child's name nor that of his family was mentioned. Yet I remember details of that broadcast now, over two decades later.

A college student at the time, I was active in my church, teaching Sunday school and leading children's worship. I didn't know when I heard the radio broadcast that the unnamed child who died was a member of my children's chapel "congregation" or that his older sister was in my high school class.

Within a few hours, though, our assistant pastor was on the phone, informing me of the tragedy. "Get over there. See them," he told me.

Why me? The family, new to our country as well as to our community, had no friends here. The assistant pastor and I were among their few acquaintances.

"I can't face those people," I replied. "Their hurt is too great. I don't know what to say. I don't know what to do."

* * *

So began my first experience of facing utterly tragic loss with others. Little did I know as I stumbled into this crisis that it would change the direction and substance of my life.

Most of the last twenty years I have been a pastor in a large Episcopal church in Beverly Hills. Earlier I ministered to a suburban congregation in Orange County, California, where I also was chaplain to a police department. In my seminary years in New York City, I served as chaplain to terminally ill children and their parents in a pediatric hospital and to incarcerated youths in a juvenile detention facility.

More recently, I've accepted an Episcopal school chaplaincy at Campbell Hall in North Hollywood, California, where I devote myself to the pastoral care of young people, their families and teachers, and to teaching the principles of caring presented in this book.

The principles of caring presented here are basic to any crisis situation we would face with a friend or loved one. I have sat with families who have lost a child. I have been with celebrities who, while outwardly successful, were facing deep personal struggles. Every day now I counsel young people through troubling problems. I share these experiences with you in the hope that you will build on your own personal qualities of caring and be better equipped to respond when someone you love faces crisis or loss.

Actually, knowing what to say or do is only one of the many issues you face in a crisis. At least as important is who you are as a person and how you can find the inner strength to stand by someone you love in times of pain and turmoil. We can be of amazing support to those close to us in their times of crisis and loss. Though we can offer much in words and action, we have even more to give them by our presence, our being with them through the pain.

There is an old saying: "Who you are speaks so loudly I cannot hear what you are saying!" Indeed, many friends and would-be helpers do good *in spite of* what they say or do during a crisis! Their love and concern is so evident that we forgive them their tactless words or clumsy actions.

Responding to friends in crisis means, first, responding as a friend. So the traits and techniques of friendship, of developing caring relationships, are the foundation for learning how to help in crisis situations. The relationship is not only the channel through which we send our help; its expression is often the most significant and therapeutic help we have to offer a friend in despair.

Almost half of the chapters that follow (Parts I and II) deal with the development of a caring personality. Other chapters explain how to understand and respond to specific crises. As you develop the caring person inside you by responding to difficult situations, every loving relationship in your life will be enhanced.

If I were to single out the most important tool of caring, it would be listening. Each of us has a need to be heard by at least one other person. If, magically, I could bestow a gift on every relationship, it would be the ability to listen. I am certain that millions of families would be healed, friendships enhanced, workplaces happier, our world made more peaceful. It has been said that "attentiveness is the rarest and purest form of generosity."[1] Effective listening is a gift, an expression of generosity so many of our hurting family members and friends long for.

To help effectively, you will also need knowledge—basic knowledge of the grief process, of specific crises, and of actions you can take.

To care for someone who is hurting, you need to understand her emotional state. Chapter 5 describes the range of emotions elicited by tough and tragic times.

Knowledge about the particular crisis affecting your loved one will help you to understand what he or she is saying and feeling. Part III deals with these specific situations, such as the death of a child, financial crises, and terminal illness. Although this book will not make you an expert on these issues, it offers a basic understanding that can help you communicate with your loved one. And your knowledge about crisis situations will also help you eliminate some of your fear of the unknown.

One note of caution: By reading this book, you will not learn enough to say to a hurting person, "I know exactly how you feel." No amount of study can provide that kind of knowledge. Even if you have been through the same kind of situation, your emotional response will have been different. But having knowledge of a crisis will help you be more sensitive to another's needs because you'll have a better idea of the complexity of the issue.

Another set of tools for caring are the resources available to help you help your loved one. Many individuals, groups, and organizations are ready to offer support in various kinds of crisis situations.

Throughout the book I describe many practical ways to show you care. You may follow them as directions or use them to stimulate your own creative juices about ways to help. Above all, I pray that reading this book encourages you, gives you confidence, and prepares you to exercise your compassion and love when someone close to you needs you most.

What to say? What to do? Often there isn't a thing left to say or do. But you can share your greatest gift— *yourself*—despite your feelings of helplessness and inadequacy. You can violate every prescribed precept of caring and still be of immeasurable aid when you manifest love, faith, loyalty, sensitivity, perseverance, courage, and integrity as you stand by your friend or loved one. Best of all, you will grow, and your relationships will deepen, as you respond to those you love in times of greatest need.

A final word of introduction, about terminology and examples. I have used *friend, family member, relative, loved one,* and similar expressions interchangeably; feel free to substitute as your own situation merits. Also, in terms of gender, I have tried to balance my use of *he, she, him,* and *her*; I aspire to be a sensitive author as well as a caring friend. When appropriate, I have used composites of similar experiences or changed names to protect the privacy of the persons who have trusted me in vulnerable moments of their lives.

# PART I

# Becoming More Responsive to Those You Care About

# 1

## Be Aware of Your Own Feelings

Since childhood, I've been afraid of hospitals and doctors. Obviously, this fear would have severely handicapped my pastoral work with sick people. So, in seminary, when it came time for my mandatory "Clinical Pastoral Education" experience, I chose a hospital setting.

The first week of the program, I was invited to sit in the "theater" overlooking the operating table. I was petrified. I refused to talk about the upcoming experience at home. I wouldn't even think about it. Afraid of getting nauseated, I even skipped breakfast the morning of the surgery. When the time came, however, I watched, fascinated, as surgeons opened the chest of a patient and replaced the heart valve. Not only did I survive the experience, I delighted in describing it all to my wife at dinner in graphic detail. Then *she* couldn't eat!

That summer's clinical experience was challenging for me, filled with the pain and hard work that accompanies growth. By facing up to my fear of hospitals, I gained the skills and knowledge I needed to work with hurting people.

## Watching Your Emotional Responses

During a crisis, you may focus so much on your hurting loved one that you forget to watch your own emotional responses. Yet being aware of your own weaknesses and emotions improves your ability to relate to others, especially when they are upset or vulnerable. Without that awareness, your emotions can cause you to turn away from a friend at a time of great need, to push your way inappropriately into a crisis, or to stand back indecisively.

Your emotions have been conditioned by experience, by your culture, and by significant others in your life. You may have to confront and counter some of your emotional conditioning in order to express your caring love to a relative in crisis. When you challenge yourself to reach out to another, you not only help someone in his time of need, but you also grow emotionally.

## Some General Thoughts About Emotions

- Your emotions are natural, human, powerful, positive attributes of your personality.

- Emotionally secure, "together" people make stable, helpful, caring friends, especially in times of crisis.

- Emotionally secure people, by definition, are in touch with their emotions. They know, understand, and accept their feelings.

- Fear of emotion creates a major barrier to interpersonal dialogue.[1]

- You take your emotions with you wherever you go. They are constantly part of you, whether you are conscious of them or not.

- Expect your emotions to be affected by the emotional outpouring of a friend, but don't take personally an outpouring of strong feelings in the midst of a crisis.

- Emotional exhaustion during a personal tragedy exceeds physical tiredness in both intensity and recovery time. The helping friend or loved one also experiences emotional fatigue.

## Your Feelings of Self-Protection

The human mind contains intricate and sophisticated mechanisms to protect it from too much stressful data. These defense mechanisms can cause us to deny bad news. In fact, denial is one of our first and strongest responses to a crisis.[2]

Even children cope with bad news by blocking its reality. For example, as a child my wife used to pretend that dead animals along the roadside were merely napping. She demonstrated another method of denial when one of her siblings was vomiting—she covered her ears tightly with her hands and sang a cheery song at the top of her lungs.

Often we are right to protect ourselves and to care first for our own needs and the needs of our immediate family. Not long ago, my father died following a massive stroke. At that time I first helped my mother, wife, and young sons through our great loss. I also cared for myself, taking time out for a few days to rest and grieve. I knew that if I didn't renew my own strength, I wouldn't be able to care effectively for others. Only after some time passed could I again reach out beyond my own family to help others.

Before we can care for others, we must be strong and healthy ourselves. A picture of that priority happens every time an airplane takes off—flight attendants instruct parents in an emergency to put oxygen masks on themselves before helping their young children to put them on.[3] To be most effective in helping and caring for others, we generally must take care of ourselves first.

In the face of a friend's crisis, not all self-protection is self-centered or inappropriate. If you wonder whether you are holding back for the wrong reasons, ask yourself these questions:

*Are my feelings coming from a lack of confidence?* The more difficult the crisis, the more likely you may be to hold back. Yet also more likely is greater pain for your loved one who stands alone. Like jumping off the high dive, committing yourself to stand by friends in times of crisis or loss becomes less intimidating after the first time and with each succeeding experience. If your reluctance is coming from a lack of faith in yourself, screw up your courage and take the plunge! Growth in self-confidence in every part of life is the result of your increasing effectiveness in caring for and loving others.

**Are my feelings of self-protection the result of cultural conditioning?** Our culture's denial of death hinders our ability to deal with crises. We think of death as an onerous monster rather than the natural end of life. As a result most Americans fear death. We hate to think about death, to plan for our deaths, to answer children's questions about death, to attend funerals, to visit with terminally ill patients, to deal with issues of aging, to visit retirement homes and hospitals, to face virtually anything that reminds us of our mortality. Our culture has even changed the vocabulary of death. People don't die; they "pass away." The effect that our cultural dread of death has had on you may hold you back from helping a friend in crisis.

Your attitude toward crises can also be affected by subcultures, such as your ethnic or religious background. I noted the influence of a religious subculture when one of my friends commented on a tiny child who was severely handicapped: "According to my religion, her parents did something wrong, and her condition is the result."

Subcultures may have affected your perception of other forms of human suffering. I have known people who view alcoholism not as a disease but as the result of moral weakness, or who believe AIDS is God's punishment of homosexuals. You should examine your beliefs to determine how strong judgments such as these influence the way you approach others in their time of need.

*Am I afraid to get involved because of emotional scars from past experiences?* Whenever you love someone, you risk that your love will go unrequited. As a chaplain to young people, I encounter many broken adolescent hearts. The pain of rejection and separation does not stop when a teenager reaches young adulthood. The scars from distant hurts you've experienced can stay with you for a long time. Stored in unconscious memory, the poor self-esteem and low self-confidence resulting from childhood abuse, for instance, can keep you from risking loving someone.

If you are immobilized by fear when facing a friend's hurt, you may suffer from a fear of intimacy, the result of old emotional wounds. Yet without intimate relationships, you can never know the freedom of being emotionally open and honest. You will never feel the joy of being accepted, valued, and embraced for being your true self. Dr. Paul Tournier, an eminent Swiss psychiatrist, wrote that none of us can become a full human person unless there is at least one other person with whom we can let down our defenses and be our true selves, totally honest and open.[4] The lack of such intimate and fulfilling relationships is what keeps many a counselor busy.

If you are feeling immobilized by fears of being rejected, overwhelmed, or taken over, you may be feeling the weight of the emotional baggage of past hurts. Be encouraged! The same crises that stir these fears within you may also provide the best setting for you to face and fight them. One of my favorite Episcopal bishops had a fear of heights. He especially disliked flying, which he needed to do often in his ministry. To conquer his fear on its own turf, he became a licensed airplane pilot!

I urge you to wade into troubled waters to help buoy up a struggling friend or loved one, even if initially you have to carry your emotional baggage on your back— most of that baggage floats! The good news is that some of the baggage will actually float away in the tide of the needs of those we care about.

## Your Personal Emotional Needs

We all need to be needed. For many of us, this need draws us to crises. Particular issues resulting from crises in our own lives also drive some of us to help others in similar situations. Some of these personal emotional needs, however, hinder us from responding effectively to a person in crisis; others assist us in helping others.

Some of your personal needs may be detrimental to your caring for another. When the need to be needed— rather than the needs of a friend in crisis—is the driving force of your involvement, slow down and reorient yourself. Otherwise you risk centering the attention on yourself (and all your good efforts), rather than on the hurting person.

A person who needs to be needed tends to take charge of everything herself, whether or not she is the right person for the task. In some cases, this attitude could prove deadly. Someone who tries on her own to care for a suicidal friend, for example, could be making a fatal mistake; she should refer that friend to a professional counselor immediately.

It's normal to need to feel needed, useful, and

valued by the people you love. Should that need turn into a hunger for the troubles of others, though, you may have problems of your own that you need to address before you attempt to reach out to another.

We Americans seem to crave drama otherwise missing in our daily lives. Many of us watch soap operas daily. Some of us even call 900-numbers to share our troubles and listen to other people's secrets. In real life, however, using the hurts of others to satisfy our need for drama is inappropriate. When you respond to a crisis, ask yourself if you are moved by the desire to gratify your own needs rather than by the urgency of compassion for a hurting friend.

Some people delight in getting a "scoop"—being the first to have news to share. As the first person to broadcast tragic news, this individual becomes a powerful and important person in the lives of those receiving the news. Other people love the power of possessing confidential information. Although they may keep the information itself confidential, they let their friends know that they know something—again, to experience a feeling of power: "I know such and such about so and so, but I can't tell you. It's a secret only I can know." But people who play with information forget that trust is a sacred part of any close relationship, and by breaking trust they may do irreparable damage to the friendship.

Some personal needs may help you reach out to a hurting loved one. In fact, part of your recovery from certain difficulties may necessitate your helping people who are facing similar difficulties. Step Twelve of Alcoholics Anonymous requires that the alcoholic assist others struggling with alcoholism. In my Beverly Hills pastoral ministry, any time a parishioner contacted me about his drinking problem, I referred him to my friend George Roosevelt, who was a descendant of Teddy Roosevelt. George enjoyed decades of sobriety through A.A. and would break his anonymity especially if he could help another person. Whenever I apologized to George for the inconvenience, he pleasantly cut off my apology, thanking me for the referral. As he told me, he needed to help other alcoholics to keep sober himself.

I still marvel when someone who has suffered terribly himself reaches out to others in a similar plight. A father who lost a daughter to suicide seeks out a family facing a similar loss. A woman who suffered a radical mastectomy years ago (and who must keep the information secret because of her career as an actress) readily shares the experience with an acquaintance about to undergo similar surgery. The personal need to reinforce our own healing by helping another is appropriate and helps guide us to assist others.

Be careful, however, that your study of an issue doesn't take precedence over actually helping the suffering friend. An episode of "M*A*S*H*" relates how military surgeon Dr. Charles Winchester, struggling with the idea of his own mortality, bombards a dying young soldier with questions. He is not thinking of alleviating the pain of the young man, but of relieving his own fear of death. Take care not to let your own intense experiences, needs, and feelings cause you to exploit the crisis of another rather than motivate you to be helpful and attentive.

## Should You Get Involved?

Monitoring your own ego needs helps you respond sensitively and appropriately in a crisis situation. To help you monitor yourself, ask yourself these four questions:

*Was I invited in?* The invitation may be merely notification. Your best friend's mother calls: "Sally asked that I especially let you know that she is in the hospital with possible pneumonia." Sally is saying to you, "Help, I need you here with me."

Sometimes the cues are subtler. When visiting a hospitalized friend recovering from a broken hip, for instance, you notice that she brightens immediately as soon as she sees you and invites you to sit down. This is an obvious invitation to stay and visit. If she is in such pain that she can barely talk to you, however, or if she seems tired and unresponsive, keep your visit very brief. People indicate that they want you or need you in different ways, according to their personality and temperament. Interpreting their signs requires varying degrees of skillfulness and sensitivity on your part.

*Does the nature of our relationship call for my involvement?* If the person in trouble is a close relative, you must help whether you want to or not—like if you learn that your teenage son is using cocaine. You're going to step into the crisis whether or not you want to and whether or not *he* wants you to. On the other hand, if the person in trouble is a distant friend or acquaintance, you may need to hold back in a crisis. After careful consideration, for example, you may tiptoe into the crisis of your life-long rival, who faces a public financial scandal—and be ready to tiptoe out again if your presence makes him uncomfortable. Some people in your life may have no one but you to care for them; the nature of your relationship with them implies your taking action when they find themselves in crisis situations.

*Does the nature of the crisis call for my involvement?* Is this the kind of situation to which you must respond? You learn, perhaps by accident, that someone close to you is distressed to the point of contemplating hurting himself or another person. Or the child who lives next door reveals to you that a parent is abusing her. In times like these, the crisis itself demands your involvement—although your involvement may be brief. In the scenarios mentioned above, your first action should be to seek expert, professional help and relegate yourself to a minor, supportive role.

*What do my instincts say?* Personal intuition is usually a reliable guide for caring persons. Your caring instincts help you decide both the quantity and quality of your involvement in the crisis of a friend. It's common sense to tread slowly and note the response to your assistance before advancing further.

You will grow emotionally as you share tough times with people you care about. Not only that, the quality of every relationship in your life will benefit from the experience of reaching out to help others. Your sensitivity will mature as you experience the hard moments in your own life and in the lives of others. People who cannot face harsh reality tend to be superficial emotionally and gloss over the needs of others in a crisis. You have chosen not to be such a "fair-weather friend," or you wouldn't have read this far. You have chosen to courageously and assertively face your own feelings, to be guided but not handicapped by them.

Feelings and instincts—what some psychologists call intuition—are invaluable in learning to care for others. In fact, intuition is often crucial to my relationships and work. Often my "third ear" picks up things that my other senses miss. Recently I felt drawn to a colleague I hadn't talked with in some months. "You've been on my mind a lot the last few days," I said. "Is everything going okay?" "Things are really bad," he replied, "and I'd appreciate the chance to talk." Developed through years of experience, your care-giving instincts will help you discover needs of others you might have never known otherwise.

I believe you can learn to trust your instincts and your feelings as you care for people around you. As you make yourself available to friends and loved ones in times of crisis and loss, your emotional strength and your sensitivity will grow—and with that growth, all the important relationships in your life will also grow.

# —— 2 ——

# Act

This year, a few days short of his seventy-eighth birthday, my father died unexpectedly while visiting in our home. Overcome with shock, numbness, and exhaustion, I lived in a fog the first few days after his death. Yet I clearly recall the helpful actions of caring friends during those days.

The cards, letters, and memorial tributes we received are still in a basket on the floor next to my nightstand. Teachers and administrators at both our boys' schools sensitively reached out to all of us. Friends shared with us thoughts or experiences that had helped them through similar loss. An acquaintance of my wife came by with a bottle of wine. An aunt called from out of state yearning to help in the kitchen: "I don't know what else I could do; I'd sure like to be there and cook for you." Though she couldn't come, food did arrive— from various quarters and in abundance! Many told us

of their prayers—we were upheld by an interdenomina-
tional and interfaith spiritual support network.

We have been blessed on every side, and we are
grateful. I would do you a disservice, however, if I didn't
express how hurt I feel that several close friends and
relatives didn't respond to our loss at all. Anyone who
has lost a loved one knows this feeling. Intellectually
and psychologically I understand the difficulty many
have dealing with death, and I bear no grudge. But on
the emotional level, I hurt, and my relationship with
those folks is significantly strained. I am especially hurt
by the silence of people whom I have helped in similar
situations.

When those dear to you face crisis or loss, your
timely response counts. Yet, having said that, let me
complicate the issue.

We Americans are action-oriented. Noted psychologist and teacher, John Bradshaw, says we risk becoming "human doings" instead of human beings.[1] We
usually need to "do" something in response to crisis—
our own crisis or that of someone close to us. We may
keep busy to avoid the crisis, or we may try to "fix"
whatever is wrong. The former is foolhardy; the latter,
frustrating. For most crisis situations are not easily fixed,
and our words and actions usually change nothing.

Instead of avoiding or fixing a crisis, then, you do
most when you simply enter and share the pain of your
friend and help her through it. That requires a lot of
strength, a significant investment of time, and specific
actions.

Although you cannot fix anything, what you *do*
counts. Even the smallest act of kindness helps.

Responding in some tangible way is as important for the doer (you), as for your friend. Indeed, your relationship may depend on it.

Here are general suggestions for actions to take in a crisis situation.

### Respond Early

Unfortunately, in a major crisis, many people hold back. Do these people genuinely believe that they will "disturb" their friend or relative by calling or writing? Do they think avoidance and neglect are virtues?

No. Most likely they are simply afraid of facing an unfamiliar issue. Afraid of encountering the raw emotions of pain and fear in another. Afraid of their own emotional response. Afraid of saying the wrong words. In fear they hold back until "the right time" or "the right setting" to reach out. They postpone doing or saying anything until so much time passes that they feel embarrassed to convey concern so late or feel dread that their caring and concern might somehow "recreate" the crisis all over again.

All the while, the suffering friend wonders what happened to the people she had always counted on for love and support. A major catastrophe has hit hard, and some significant friends and relatives haven't even bothered to make the tiniest communication.

Relationships change in time of crisis and loss. Relationships deepen as we stand by one another through the hard times. Relationships suffer and even die when we neglect those who need us at such times.

Respond early. Guided by your own comfort level,

logistics, and other aspects of your situation and that of your friend in crisis, get in touch right away. How?

- Call on the telephone.
- Visit in person.
- Send a card.
- Write a note.

What should you convey? Tell him that you just heard what happened. Be specific: "I just learned that your brother died." Say how you feel: "I'm shocked and hurt." Offer your assistance: "I want to help you in any way I can." Don't be overly concerned at this point about content. You are communicating your love and caring by getting in touch, no matter what the words. Even the tackiest greeting card conveys that you are thinking about your loved one, that you went to the trouble to find a card for him, and that you want to communicate your love.

In the basket beside my nightstand are dozens of sympathy cards. I can't tell you the printed greeting on a single one, but I remember the thoughtful friends and loved ones who wanted to be in touch with me about the death of my father.

Recently, a friend who was recovering from a number of stressful crises didn't know how to respond to the death of a beloved aunt. He hadn't communicated in years with her children and, due to his own situation, couldn't get to the funeral. He was struggling with how to respond to his cousins. I suggested that he call each of them, and I stuck around as he made the calls. Much to his surprise, the calls went well. Within hours of his aunt's death, he'd reestablished relationships and helped both his cousins and himself feel better. With some help, my friend got over the hump of reluctance and avoidance. Today he still enjoys his renewed relationships with his cousins.

### Ideas for Caring Actions

A dear, older friend of ours used to keep several T-bone steaks, individually wrapped, in white butcher paper in her freezer. When a neighbor was ill or dealing with a crisis of some kind, our friend would tie a festive ribbon around one of those packaged steaks and deliver it with a note. Your caring actions toward others are limited only by your creativity and capabilities. And they may be delicious!

Once I asked a group of high-school students to brainstorm possible responses to a family in their neighborhood dealing with the sudden serious illness of either the husband or wife. In moments they suggested: telephoning, sending a card, writing a note, visiting to keep them company, being there to listen, taking flowers or other gifts, organizing friends in the neighborhood to help with food and other needs, offering financial help, running errands, cooking, and taking care of trivial jobs. If the family was younger and with little children, baby-sitting was added to the list. For a household of elderly members, the students suggested helping with heavy work or shopping.

Following is a list of helpful actions that can help someone who is facing a crisis. Choose actions that seem appropriate to the situation—or let this list stimulate your thinking to come up with a caring action all your own. Before you do anything, however, pray for guidance to do the right thing, and listen for cues that would indicate what would help.

Write a note.

Send a card.

Send flowers.

Call on the telephone.

Send them postcards when you are on a trip.

Take a flower from your garden.

Take fruit or vegetables from your garden.

Take a portion of a special meal or dessert you've prepared for your family.

Telephone before going grocery shopping to check for needs.

Wash their car.

Mow their lawn.

Have your children draw a picture or make a card and deliver it.

Buy a card for a group to sign.

Gather funds as needed and appropriate.

Prepare a casserole for them to freeze for a future meal.

Ask if you can let their pastor know of their need.

Ask if you can place their name on a prayer list of a congregation or group.

Take letters or packages to the post office.

Get information on local support groups.

Invite them to your home for lunch or dinner.

Take them out for a meal.

Give them a tape or CD of their favorite music.

Give them a book by their favorite author.

Cook and deliver a complete meal.

Organize others to provide meals.

Telephone them while you are on an extended trip.

Make telephone calls for them.

Answer their telephone during their time of loss.

Help children with homework.

Drive children to school and other activities.

Call to check in when you get home at night.

Bake them some cookies.

Check on them during a storm or heat wave or natural disaster.

Send a friendship card or note weekly.

Remember their birthday, holidays, and other special times.

Water their yard.

Walk their dog.

Invite them to join you on a special occasion.

Cook something on their new special diet and deliver it.

Take parcels and newspapers to their door.

Send comforting and inspirational news clippings (no preaching, advice, or cures).

Write a newsy letter over several days.

Send photographs of special experiences.

Send a plant.

Plant their vegetable garden.

Send dried fruit.

Send a special assortment of teas.

Mail small gifts periodically.

Play ball with their children.

Baby-sit their children.

Take their clothes to the laundry or dry cleaner.

Sit quietly with them in the hospital.

Clean their house.

Pick up relatives at the airport or return them.

Put up out-of-town guests in your home.

Go to the video store to get them a movie.

Invite them to your house to watch a big game or special video.

Drive them to church.

Help arrange their own club, study, or prayer group to meet at their house.

See if they would like to ride along while you do errands.

Take your children for brief visits, especially on holidays.

Send a tribute contribution to their favorite charity.

Deliver a pie or cake.

Take them to an inspirational exhibit at an art museum.

Drive them to the library to choose a book.

Send a copy of a favorite poem.

Send a poem you've composed yourself.

## When to Act

When should you act? How long should you help out? The nature of the crisis and the closeness of your relationship helps determine what to do over the short- and long-term. Since my father's death, virtually every day I've known my mother to be home alone, I've briefly checked in with her. I expect that will be helpful to her (and to me) for at least a year or so, especially since so many of her friends and relatives have stopped calling.

Don't forget that some crises may last months or

even years. The same kind of responses that you made when you originally heard of the crisis—the phone calls, visits, cards, and letters—in many cases may be appropriate for several months, even a year or more.

In conclusion, act early to keep communication open and your relationship alive. Provide helpful assistance, and stand beside your friend or relative. Once you are with the one you care about, you can express compassion and love even greater than words and actions can express, not by *doing for* but by *being with* him or her, committed and enduring.

## —— 3 ——

## *Be*

One night a small boy, troubled with nightmares, cried out for his father. The father came to his room, talked to him, hugged him reassuringly, and tucked him in. But no sooner had he returned to his bed than his son called out again. This time the father turned on a night-light and left the bedroom door open. His son still wasn't comforted, however. Finally, the father sat on the bed next to his son and said, "Don't be afraid. You're not alone—God is here."

The little boy thought about this. Then, looking up at his father, he said, "Yeah, but right now I think I need someone with skin on."[1]

### Being Present

The highest expression of caring is not so much in what we say or do as it is in *where* and *who* we are.

When we hurt, we need "someone with skin on" to stay with us.

In our increasingly high-tech society, says John Naisbitt in *Megatrends*, we grow hungrier and hungrier for intimacy. Naisbitt labels this trend "High Tech High Touch."[2] We need to be close to people. We need to be with people who care about us, who cherish us.

In the words of a popular song, those we care about need to know that "whenever you need me, I'll be there." This phrase touches the heart of Christian faith. Before he ascended into heaven, Jesus said to his followers, "I will be with you always" (Matthew 28:20).

When I worked with terminally ill children and their families, I learned that caring often means simply *being present*. No matter how helpless you may feel in responding to a crisis, you can help immeasurably by simply *being with your loved one*.

Love is the ultimate reality and the greatest gift. When we love someone, more than anything else we want to be with that person. The nature of the activity or the quality of the conversation is not important. Indeed, the presence of one we love can transform even the most common actions or words into a special moment. Sitting quietly together can be some of the greatest "quality time" we can spend with someone we care about.

My early hospital visits drove home to me the importance of being present with people in times of crisis. On one such visit I arrived before dawn to sit with a neighbor who was about to undergo a major operation. Alone and frightened, she readily accepted my offer to stay with her until she was taken to the operating room. Once she was medicated, I sat quietly while she relaxed and rested her eyes. She never forgot that visit, which cemented our friendship for life. What mattered to her and what she always remembered was my presence with her at a time of emotional need. I was there.

The second visit didn't go according to plan. An elderly parishioner went into surgery earlier than scheduled, and I arrived as she was being brought back to her bed from the recovery room. Though I advise you not to visit a hospital patient within twenty-four hours after surgery, except under unusual circumstances, this visit turned out to be helpful. As she opened her eyes, there I was. She told me that I was her "angel" (the effects of general anesthesia, no doubt!). Most surgery patients don't remember much of the hours after a major operation, but she never forgot that "angelic" vision. It wasn't anything profound that I did or said; my *being there* was what mattered.

Of course, "being there" requires time and commitment. Even more, it requires us to overcome our fears of an unfamiliar or uncomfortable setting, such as a hospital. Yet I know of nothing that better expresses our care and love, especially in the most tragic moments of crisis and loss.

You don't know what to say? You don't know what to do? *Be there!*

## Be the Whole You

Be there. Be yourself. Develop the personality with which you are gifted. The following seven phrases characterize how a caring person should *be*.[3]

**Be a person.** A caring person is authentic, unique, and gifted—that's *you*. Be who you are. In *The Meaning of Persons*, Dr. Tournier contrasted the true person inside each of us with the roles we play or masks we wear. Often we wear so many masks that not only do others fail to know who we are, we're not even sure who we are ourselves![4]

Early in my seminary years in New York City, I served as a part-time chaplain in a juvenile detention facility. It was a difficult setting in which to offer pastoral care. Most of my "parishioners" were impoverished, hardened teenagers from the toughest ghetto neighborhoods. To get in to see them, I used a huge jail key. Although other care givers experienced numerous problems with the kids (one dormitory counselor was brutally attacked one evening when he tried to identify with the youths as "one of the gang"), I don't recall a single problem with any of the youngsters I visited.

One evening near the end of my year of service, one of the counselors told me why I hadn't had any problems with the kids: "You've been effective here," he said, "even if you're really square! You've been yourself. These kids respect that. They can see right through a phony who is trying to be one of them."

Any accomplishments I've felt good about and anything good that has happened to me, including my marriage of over two decades, have come when I have been true to my authentic person, warts and all.

The first attribute of a caring person is to *be a person*.

***Be in dialogue with others.*** Dialogue, encounter, communication, and relationship all define two-way experiences characterized by trust and openness. A caring person listens at least as much as he or she talks—and probably more.

Being authentic as a person begins with knowing who you are. Interpersonal relationship means two authentic persons in dialogue with one another. Many of us, afraid that others will not tolerate our honesty, settle for superficial relationships.

A caring person builds, through conversation, the kind of relationship with others that stands the test of tough times. A caring relationship is a meaning-full relationship in which you have shared meaning with those you care about. Trust is a by-product of that relationship.

We've all experienced what happens when relationships lack the quality of authentic dialogue. Mr. and Mrs. Jones, the story goes, once had such a heated quarrel that they weren't speaking to each other. At bedtime Mr. Jones scrawled a note and propped it against the alarm clock on the nightstand before stomping off to sleep on the living room sofa. The note read, "Let me know when it's 7:00 a.m." The next morning he woke up, looked at his watch, and saw it was already 8:30! He stormed up the stairs to his bedroom. There, propped up alongside the alarm clock, was a new note. It read, "It's 7:00 a.m."

Open dialogue creates a structure upon which two persons build a caring relationship. Without dialogue you cannot know or respond to the needs of others effectively.

*Be self-disclosing.* In our most fulfilling relationships, we share from the heart. Each of us is an awesome mystery to those around us, even to our intimates (perhaps even to ourselves!). Although this mystery of our true being makes knowing each other an exciting adventure, unless we "lift the curtain" on our thoughts and feelings, the mystery cannot be solved by those who want to be close to us. Many marriages disintegrate because personal aspirations, needs, and feelings are not disclosed.

Disclosing our deepest feelings may not be appropriate in the midst of another person's trauma. But mutual trust will grow over time in an atmosphere of honest sharing and vulnerability.

To create relationships in which we may care for others and in which they may care for us requires self-disclosure. On a recent flight, I began some small talk with the man seated next to me. "What do you do?" we asked each other in turn. When he learned that I was a school chaplain, he asked, "How are the children from divorced families doing at your school?" Soon we were sharing from our hearts about parenting and our aspirations for our children; then he opened up about his recent and painful divorce.

In my theological studies, I learned of a special moment in the divine-human relationship called a "blick." The burning bush provided a "blick" for Moses, opening up and deepening his relationship with God. Similarly, our times of human self-disclosure hold the potential to be a "blick," opening a door in our relationship with another person.

Our power to relate to others is analogous to the

Almighty's. Knowledge of God is called "revelation," because we only know about God what he "reveals" or "unveils." In the same way, what others know about us and how close we grow together rests in our own power to lift the veil.

*Be understanding.* Understanding means receiving the self-disclosure of another person. Understanding means listening with the heart. The man who asks, "Why?" at the deathbed of his wife is not asking for some boiled-down philosophy or theology, but for someone to hear his hurt and stand by him in his grief.

We turn others off when we fail to understand, to listen with our heart. Each of us needs to be truly heard, to be understood, by at least one other human being if we are to develop fully. If you were to listen to all the conversations of the world, between nations as well as those between couples, they would sound for the most part like dialogues of creatures without ears.

I've had many experiences in crisis counseling when people ask questions for which I have no answers. Often these questions are an expression of the anger and hurt of grief. We can help the healing process if we listen and try to understand hurt people without becoming defensive or answer-bound.

*Be a model of a person "on the road."* From watching my sons, I know that an elementary school baseball field is a wonderful laboratory for observing human behavior. Every player is simultaneously a captain, a coach, and an umpire. Everyone is an expert on the game, a master of even the most obscure rules, and capable of perfect judgment calls no matter how far away their position from the action.

As we grow older, however, our judgments become more cautious. My professors used to tell me that the more I learned, the more I would learn how much I didn't know. The same principle is true in matters of the heart—in knowing yourself and in knowing others.

Becoming an adult means having more questions than answers; it means realizing that the essence of our lives is more in the journey than in the destination. When we are willing to acknowledge how unfathomable knowledge is, then we have reached intellectual, emotional, and spiritual maturity.

When others see in you a model of a person "on the road"—on pilgrimage, becoming, growing, and changing—they are drawn to you. When their going gets rough, they will want you to walk with them.

**Be trustworthy.** Some of my high school students once studied friendship as part of a psychology unit in a health class. When they compiled their definitions of friendship, trust was at the top of the list.

When I confide in a close friend, I trust that he or she will (1) listen attentively and focus on what I am revealing about myself, (2) accept me as a person and accept my feelings without judging me, even if he or she disagrees with my words or actions, and (3) keep confidential sharing confidential.

People incapable of keeping confidences quickly stop receiving them. A professional colleague of mine is unable to keep personal information about others confidential. The word of such a personality weakness spreads quickly. Few confide in her anymore.

*Confidential* does not mean the same thing as keeping secrets, although that is part of confidentiality. *Confidential* means having confidence in someone's discernment and judgment. Normally that means the confidant does not even intimate knowledge of someone's personal problem to others. Although in rare circumstances, which I define in chapter 15, we may have to get the friend to expert help even if he has asked us to maintain secrecy.

**Be caught up in love.** I recall reading of a nun caring for terminally ill patients in a hospice. A visitor observed her cleaning up a patient who had just vomited. "I wouldn't do your job for a million dollars," said the visitor. Looking up from the sickly patient, the nun replied: "Neither would I."

There is nothing more powerful or compelling than love—no amount of compensation, no force of nature, no political movement, no popular success. Love is stronger than any other force.

As we tap into the power of love, God increases our ability to love. He enables us to love unconditionally, with no strings attached. He helps us to accept and forgive, not out of weakness but with new strength. He enables us to stand by our beloved through anything.

Through twenty years of caring for people facing tragedies of all kinds, the only thing that has continuously made sense to me is love. The apostle Paul said that there are three things that remain forever: "faith, hope, and love. But the greatest of these is love" (1 Corinthians 13:13).

# PART II

# Developing Tools of Caring

# —— 4 ——

# Become an Effective Listener

I don't know of a tougher setting for responding as a caring friend than a children's cancer ward. Innocent, beautiful children are suffering—and parents are torn up with anger and frustration. The atmosphere in the face of such hurt is sometimes nearly unbearable. Yet that is where I found myself one summer when I served as a chaplain to three floors of terminally ill children and their parents in a New York City hospital.

One of the first patients I met was a two-year-old attended by his father. The little boy was suffering the advanced stages of his fatal disease. His father, who had given up every other obligation to be with his son constantly, suffered with him.

The father's rage knew no bounds. A Christian convert, he had been victimized by a television preacher who, in reply to his cry for help, sent him a form letter asking for more "seed offerings" to work a divine miracle. The father was angry at God. Since I was God's nearest representative, the anguished parent directed his wrath at me.

Every day I would literally drag myself back to that sad, sad room to face the drawn, pixie-like face of the tiny patient and the bottomless cistern of emotion of his tortured father. For most of each visit, the father would rail at me. One day he pulled back the sheet from his son's distended stomach covered with sores and screamed: "I'd like to have your God here right now! I'd push his nose into the sores on my son's stomach. Where is your God?"

The father didn't want answers to his extended, rhetorical questions. He sought someone to hear him out because he needed catharsis. He needed to release his pent-up emotions, to lance the infected wound of his spirit, to let the poison of his anger out so healing could begin. The only way I could help him was by soaking up his hurts.

No matter how long I listened, though, no matter how much I soaked up his hurt, nothing seemed to help. The father's rage did not diminish, and I felt helpless and useless. Yet I continued to come. I continued to stand at the bed of this helpless child. I continued to listen to his father's angry words.

As the end of my hospital assignment neared, the day came for me to say good-bye to the suffering father and son. I expected to be relieved to go, and I thought the angry father would be glad to see me gone. Instead, the father burst into tears, saying to his weak little one what a nice man I was, how much I'd meant to them, how they would miss me.

Some months later I learned the child died. I was told that the father's grief, while understandably severe, was not volatile. He had apparently gotten out his worst anger in anticipation of his son's death.

In this terrible tragedy, all I could do was be there and listen. If effective listening was meaningful in this most extreme situation, it certainly transmits caring and love in less volatile encounters and relationships.

## Characteristics of Active Listeners

Listening is the most important skill a caring person can develop, for effective listening is active rather than passive. It is an activity that requires energy and concentration. Yet most of us seem unprepared to listen. Most of us have problems being still. We crave sound. Schools may teach us to write and speak, requiring us to study composition and public speaking. But rarely do schools offer a class in listening.

Most of us fail to listen in everyday conversation. At worst, we tune out our friends or interrupt them. At best, we anticipate what a friend is going to say and make our conclusions before she has finished talking; or we may use the time she is speaking to prepare our own retort, even though we may not have fully received her message.

Yet we know people who listen. We call them our best friends because they listen effectively and actively. Because they draw us out and let us talk, we think they are interesting conversationalists.

Further, these same interesting conversationalists don't tell us what to do (except when they feel it's an emergency) or how to feel. They don't respond to our crises with easy answers or shallow philosophies. They don't offer us cures. They don't preach at us. They know themselves and their limitations. They are comfortable with their own emotions and are secure in hearing ours. Their listening is often healing for us.

These effective listeners are models. Think about how an effective listener makes you feel and how they set the stage for you to express yourself freely and completely. They probably exhibit most of the characteristics of effective listening listed below.

*Ask questions to allow complete and free expression.* By custom, some questions don't ask for much of a response. If in passing a friend in a hallway at work I ask, "How are you?" or "How do you feel?" I probably mean the question as a greeting and expect a "Fine, how are you?" in response as I walk away. The meaning of my question is very different, however, if I take my cup of coffee to the lounge, sit next to my friend, look at him, ask, "How are things going for you?" and await a response. Obviously, the question in this situation calls for a more detailed reply.

Questions indicate your interest in what's being said and your desire to understand. Questions help clarify: "How do you mean?" Questions help the listener follow the discussion: "Could you repeat that? It sounds so important, and I want to understand." Often a friend in crisis needs a sounding board to sort out her feelings or to figure out different courses of action. Ask questions that help her consider options and stay on track.

Avoid questions that ask more than your friend is comfortable sharing. Avoid a rapid succession of questions—they sound more like cross-examination than sensitive dialogue.

*Reflect the feelings expressed.* As you listen and begin to sense how your friend is feeling, reflect his feelings back to him. You may say things like: "That must have made you angry"; "That hurts"; "How frightening!"; "I can tell how sad you are"; or simply "Oh, no."

By reflecting feelings the active listener expresses caring and interest and encourages the speaker to continue. Reflections also help summarize or clarify what is being said. Reflecting feelings helps you avoid giving unwanted advice and allows your friend to come to his own conclusion or course of action.

When you reflect feelings, avoid saying, "I know exactly how you feel." This sentence conveys one of four things, most of them unhelpful: (1) "I've heard enough to know what you're talking about, and I don't want to hear any more"; (2) "I don't know what you're talking about, but I have a sense of your feelings and don't want to face them with you"; (3) "That reminds me of some unresolved, awful experience in my past, and now I'm going to tell you all about it"; or (4) "I have had the same experience and remember how I felt."

The last response may be helpful if you really have had a similar experience. Yet even if you went through a similar crisis, you likely did not feel the same emotions as your friend. Also, your memory of how you felt may not be accurate. For some, pain lessens over time. For others, anguish builds through the years. Just as sensitivity to physical pain varies dramatically from person to person, so does sensitivity to emotional pain.

You may, however, say that your *experience* was similar. That's different from claiming knowledge of the same *feelings*. For instance, a woman who confides her own experience of a mastectomy to a friend facing such traumatic surgery can be a happy example of survival. Similarly, parents who lost a baby to crib death can help support other parents dealing with that tragedy. In fact, a wide variety of support groups for people who share similar problems meet regularly, such as Alcoholics Anonymous and Overeaters Anonymous. In these groups hurting people share their experiences and feelings and receive comfort from others who are battling similar problems.

As you talk about your experience, do not confuse the *experience* with your *emotional response* to that experience. You should never inhibit your friend's attempt to talk about her emotions by claiming prior knowledge of them. When you say, "I know exactly how you feel," you run the risk—however unintentional—of belittling her emotions. For, quite simply, you *can't* know how someone is feeling.

**Don't take the expression of negative feelings personally.** In the grip of a crisis, your friend may say emotionally charged things like "I hate God!" or "I'm going to divorce him as soon as I can!" You shouldn't take these negative emotions personally. Rather, you should simply listen and let your friend blow off steam. By doing so, you provide a catharsis—a chance for your friend to purge or relieve her emotions.

During such times, your friend's emotions and words may seem out of character. Some of her words may even sound like personal attacks on your character or your relationship with her. As difficult as it may be for you, don't shrink from the encounter. By listening you help your friend to drain her wounds and start her on the way to healing.

Usually people "blow off" to those they trust most in the world. You may be the trusted friend who chooses to listen to a loved one's pain. Yet loving your friend leaves you vulnerable to her outbursts. Understanding that your friend is speaking out of extreme pain protects your feelings throughout a conversation. Regularly remind yourself not to take the outburst personally.

In some situations catharsis is inappropriate, and you should gently interrupt your friend or loved one. When catharsis becomes irrational or confessional beyond the bounds of your expertise, you may need to find professional help for your friend. (In chapter 15 I discuss in more detail how to deal with times when you are in over your head.)

**Be "centered" on the person you are listening to.** Centered means focused, attentive, tuned in. Some people cannot listen effectively if they are sitting behind a desk covered with papers because their eyes and attention wander to the work on the desk and away from the speaker. Physically moving away from distraction may be necessary to these people. If one of my children wants to talk while we are driving, I turn off the radio to improve my listening. Create the optimum

environment for you to center your attention on your
friend.

Being centered on your friend also allows you to
watch for your own emotional response to him and his
situation. If you are not focused on him and his needs,
you may reveal feelings of shock, fear, or embarrassment, and silence a friend who desperately needs to talk
things out. Effective listening means being aware of how
your own feelings come into play in a particular
conversation and restraining those feelings to give your
friend the chance he needs to air his problems.

Being centered also means being aware of spoken
and unspoken cues that indicate some troubling issue.
For example, you ask a close friend how things are
going, and she replies, "Okay . . . I guess." Or she says
"Fine," but her eyes well up with tears. Or an old friend
who never telephones, calls to "check in, if you have a
few minutes." In each case, a verbal or nonverbal cue
has indicated that your friend is in need of a listening
ear.

*Be affirming and accepting of your friend or loved
one.* Even if you are anxious about an issue being raised
or an experience being related, your love for the other
person and effective listening call for affirmation and
acceptance. Accepting someone is simply responding in
such a way that your friend feels comfortable enough to
share herself with you—warts and all. Acceptance does
not necessarily include approval.

Many people feel embarrassed when sharing emotions, especially negative feelings. As a caring listener,
you "authenticate" your friend when you help him

accept his emotional response to crisis and loss. That is, you help him feel comfortable with his own emotions. We accomplish this affirmation as we listen and give brief, encouraging responses that indicate our understanding and love.

For instance, you are lunching with a dignified older friend, a widower, on what would have been his golden anniversary of marriage to his beloved who died three years ago. During the course of the meal, he breaks down. He is embarrassed by his show of emotion. As his friend, you affirm his feelings by grasping his hand and saying, "This would be a tough day for anyone in your place. I miss her too."

To most of us, an emotional response to grief is natural. Some people, however, have difficulty expressing their emotions. They need reassurance that they have not humiliated themselves nor embarrassed you. The active and caring listener allows a friend to be himself, openly and honestly.

**Work at patience as you listen.** In an age of instant electronic conveyance of information and communication, interpersonal relationships are still built the old-fashioned way—word by word, smile by smile, tear by tear. Those of us who savor friendship and conversation prefer it this way, yet often we carry our desire for instant communication into our relationships.

Active listening requires intentional patience. Patience is hard work for most of us, like holding on to the reins of a thoroughbred at the starting gate. Yet the most significant relationships are often the reward of two people each willing to "wait out" the other.

The silences in conversations are the toughest. Ever notice how hard it is to be still in the midst of an emotional discussion? We previously considered how important it is to sit quietly with another person, to be with someone special for extended periods in times of crisis and loss.

Often the most important thing is said after a time of quiet reflection or after a lot of listening. One of my parishioners once phoned and anxiously requested to meet with me that same day. She came later that afternoon, but instead of talking about her problem right away, she kept the conversation on a superficial level for some time. Finally, after a quiet lull, she burst into tears and blurted out, "I think my husband is having an affair."

You cannot "hurry" the sharing from another person's heart. Perhaps a friend is reconsidering whether or not to share a secret hurt. Perhaps she wants to determine if you really care or if you are really listening. You may have to listen through the preliminaries before she shares what she wants to entrust to you.

Patience may be the most important quality of an effective listener and caring friend. It is surely among the most difficult qualities for most of us to develop.

*"Listen" to nonverbal communication and body language.* Psychologists and communication experts have produced major studies on body language, the way people communicate without uttering a word. As the caring listener grows more observant, more patient, and more sensitive, the ability to receive and translate nonverbal messages grows.

If a friend begins staring at her watch and shifting her weight nervously from side to side, it is likely a good time to end your visit. On the other hand, if she leads you to a chair and presents a tray with food and drink, you can be certain that she wants you to sit and talk.

Being "centered" on your friend as you listen helps you receive subtle, significant, nonverbal messages. If a friend bends forward toward you in conversation, you might note in that earnest gesture that what he is about to say is of intense importance to him.

The better we know a person, the more practiced we become at "listening" to unsaid communications. In a marriage of some years, the slightest movement of a spouse's head or hand or eye may speak volumes to the partner. Intimate friends and close working associates develop similar skill at almost intuitively picking up unspoken messages.

The caring friend listens with the eyes as well as the ears, actively receiving nonverbal cues that indicate the significance of what's being said.

*Give nonverbal cues of attention.* The caring friend can send the words, "I am listening," without making a sound. He projects cues that encourage his friend to talk, as well as avoiding cues of impatience or inattentiveness.

Actions like turning down the radio when a loved one wants to talk or clearing off your desk to prepare for an important discussion communicate to your friend that "Listening to you is the most important thing I have to do." If you are listening, physical gestures of various kinds will come naturally—gestures like eye contact (no part of us better indicates the direction of our attention than our eyes) or leaning slightly forward ("listening" with your body) say in body language, "I am tuned in to what you are saying."

You have probably experienced the cues that indicate inattentiveness, and you must diligently avoid using them. The subtleties are rarely lost; most of us can hear, even by telephone, the unspoken impatience or inattention of a friend. In person, such cues of inattention are magnified.

Active listening means physically exhibiting behaviors that say how much we care.

***Know when you are over your head.*** Chapter 15 deals with your role when you know you are over your head with a friend who is in extreme crisis. But how can you know when you are over your head?

Sometimes the issue itself is beyond your ability to help. You cannot, for example, cure someone who struggles with an addiction to gambling. Nor can you alone heal someone who has been wounded by sexual abuse.

On rare occasions, the talk itself signals the need for professional assistance. If a loved one becomes incoherent or begins to share confidential information in a way you know is out of character for her, you should avoid most of the listening techniques given above that encourage emotional release. Gently and lovingly, stop the conversation. Then help your friend find professional assistance.

A warning: Just because you become uncomfortable when a friend shares a confidence does not mean she is being inappropriate. You may simply be the only person she trusts enough to tell about an issue which may indeed require professional counseling. Your hasty retreat may hinder your friend or relative from ever getting help.

For example, the first time a victim of sexual abuse confides her hurt to another is most critical—no matter what the victim's age or how far back in life the abuse occurred. The kind of response the victim receives often determines whether she will ever express her hurts again—and also whether she will ever receive professional therapeutic attention and recover.

Of course, listening to bad news from a friend can be frightening. My hope is that this book lessens your anxiety as it explains how to face some of the crises you may encounter with a friend or relative, freeing you to truly help another.

Effective, active listening is an expression and a tool of caring and sensitivity. Although I have dissected it and analyzed it, effective listening is as natural as the spontaneous conversation of friends over lunch. Improving your listening skills enhances every important relationship of your life.

# —— 5 ——

# Understand the Emotions of Grief

The emotions of grief set in motion powerful, sometimes explosive, forces within the sufferer. Holding the lid on such emotional energy is like trying to contain a powerful chemical reaction. Somehow, sometime, it's going to blow. Those closest to a grief-stricken person often underestimate the impending release of emotion, its force, and its duration.

Nine-year-old Rebecca learned at school about the death of a classmate's mother. Once at home, she cried hysterically and began to show signs of severe fear and depression. She grieved profoundly for days.

Rebecca's parents angrily blamed the school for her pain. They questioned why the teacher told the class about the death of the schoolmate's mother. The teacher explained that the students should be prepared for the grieving child to return to school, both to respond sensitively and to anticipate their own feelings, especially fear, about the death of a peer's parent. But the explanation did not placate Rebecca's angry parents, who retorted that instead of helping their daughter, the school had made her emotionally upset.

They complained to the principal, who responded by urging them to let their daughter emote, to hold her and let her cry, to draw out her feelings. No, they said, that wasn't how their family dealt with loss. In fact, they explained, they had only a few weeks before handled an even more tragic situation and contained it—and Rebecca's emotions—quite successfully. The principal asked them to tell her about it.

Rebecca's mother, her voice cracking, related how their dearest friends, a young family, former neighbors in a distant state, had suffered the deaths of the mother and two children, one of them Rebecca's best friend, in a private plane crash. Rebecca recovered quickly, her mother explained. The family discussed the loss briefly, shed a few tears, then distracted themselves by "getting on with life." The parents "toughened" Rebecca up and helped her to "get a hold of herself" when she would become weepy.

But now the school, on some "trendy psychological binge," had caused Rebecca to unravel. No telling, the parents exclaimed, how many other students the teacher and principal had damaged by setting all the emotions free. (Every other parent who called expressed appreciation and gratitude to the school for handling such a frightening loss so well.)

Rebecca's parents never understood the force of her emotions of grief: sadness for her classmate, despondence over the untimely and violent death of her best friend, unthinkable horror that a child could lose a parent and that her own mother could be similarly lost to her, and a generalized dread of death. They never recognized their own emotions of grief and couldn't allow their daughter hers.

Unaddressed, Rebecca's grief will be her life-long companion. We cannot carry such potent feelings around with us without paying the price in our mental and physical health and in our relationships with others.

## Eighteen Emotional Responses to Grief

Understanding the emotions of grief helps you respond to friends when they mourn the loss of a loved one. Similar expressions of grief also accompany the death of a relationship, the death of a lifestyle, the death of independence or security, or the anticipation of death or loss of beloved people or situations:

- A forty-year-old father of three young children learns he has a spreading cancer.

- A twenty-year-old cousin is suddenly paralyzed after a motorcycle accident.

- An aging parent faces selling the family home to enter a retirement community.

- A close friend is unexpectedly served with divorce papers after sixteen years of marriage.

- A single elderly aunt's favorite pet is struck by a car and killed.

Virtually any crisis, loss, or change of status that causes stress also triggers a grief response. You should expect the emotions of grief in these situations.

Even positive, joyful events can trigger grief:

- An only child marries someone her parents aren't quite sure of.

- Teenagers are told by their parents of a job promotion that necessitates a move thousands of miles away.

- A mother drops her firstborn off at school for the first day of kindergarten.

Grief is a complex emotional process we go through when we experience loss. Not everyone experiences all of the following eighteen emotional responses associated with grief. Not everyone experiences them in the same order. The emotions and process of grief differ in individuals even as emotional makeup differs from person to person. Some friends are reluctant to let you see their emotions; some don't let you see their grief at all. Respect their privacy and their dignity.

Yet most close friends and relatives do not suffer quietly. Hopefully, having some knowledge of what to expect will help you be more comfortable with them and embolden you to help.

**Numbness.** Initially, the mind attempts to protect itself from tragic news by shutting down to minimal functioning. Little information is received or sent. The mind desensitizes itself against emotional signals. A loved one in crisis may appear zombie-like, drugged.

Unfortunately, doctors or friends often medicate the grief-stricken person, further slowing down thought and delaying (and often complicating) the natural grieving process.

When a close relative dies, family members may be further numbed from emotions by the many details that require their attention. This initial preoccupation may preclude them from acknowledging their feelings or the loving outreach of friends.

Should you be with a relative immediately after he receives word of loss, you may find his emotional level significantly lowered. In the days and weeks ahead, however, his emotions will intensify—even if his grief is initially severe. The pain of grief usually gets worse before it gets better.

Don't conclude that your relative is "okay" on the basis of an initial response. He may simply be numb. As the days go by, he will increasingly need your loving care.

*Denial.* The mind can react to the worst news by refusing to accept it. Denial is one of the mind's most potent defense mechanisms. Hence, denial is a natural response to news of death or other tragic loss. In her important book, *On Death and Dying*, Dr. Elisabeth Kubler-Ross describes denial as the normal first response of a patient to the diagnosis of terminal illness.[1]

Especially when death or loss is sudden and unexpected, denial is a likely initial response. One of my sons, on hearing of the death of a dear older friend responded, "No! He isn't dead. I just talked to him on the phone." These words of a three-year-old could just as easily come out of the mouth of an adult ten or twenty times his age.

Denial, like numbness, wears off as reality sinks in. In the case of untimely and sudden death, confronting the body of a loved one forces a person to deal with reality. Sometimes a pastor or counselor must push that confrontation so that, mercifully, the grief process that leads to recovery can begin.

Not long ago, one of my best friends died in an automobile accident. Because of the severity of injuries, the mortuary advised the family against viewing her body. Her son, in his twenties, asked me to identify his mother's body for him. His request indicated his insight about his own denial and the need for someone he trusted to confront him with the finality of his mother's death.

If you have a friend going through denial, stand by him till it passes. Denial that persists and becomes emotionally inappropriate may indicate that your friend needs professional help to accept reality. Your friend will need you increasingly as he accepts reality more and more.

*Indecisiveness.* Grief, like any emotional trauma, weakens the mind's decision-making faculties. Often in my counseling I have urged people to make decisions when they feel strong, rested, and in good spirits. For that reason I urge those grieving the death of a loved one to postpone for a year or more all major decisions possible—like selling a home or moving.

This counsel is not always practical. The tragic and untimely death of someone close forces many persons into immediate and major decisions. Further, in most cases the death of a family member demands immediate decisions, beginning with funeral arrangements. Unfortunately, many don't keep their personal affairs in order well enough to relieve their families of difficult decisions and plans when they need it most.

My most extreme experience with trauma-related indecisiveness occurred when a friend discovered the body of his grown son alongside his rifle. Instead of dialing 911, he phoned me to ask what to do next! I immediately instructed him to call the paramedics and police, action which in other circumstances would have come natural to him. His response was understandable in the face of such tragedy; he just didn't know what to do.

Because a person in severe grief is indecisive, caring relatives and friends should observe a fine line between helpful guidance for immediate problems (calling for help; direction to legal, medical, and pastoral assistance) and inappropriate meddling and manipulation (pushing advice, rushing decisions that may be postponed or which should be discussed with others). A bereaved friend may be overly open to suggestion in many big decisions. When hit in the face with divorce action, for instance, a wife may agree in the shock and depression of the moment to make concessions that she later regrets.

When you are aware of your friend's inability to make decisions due to her grief, become more sensitive to her needs, helping her without imposing your will.

*Hypersensitivity.* One moment your grief-stricken friend may be numb and zombie-like. The next moment she may lash out over the smallest of issues. Such a dramatic reversal may seem surprising, but such is grief. Over time, a friend or relative suffering a great loss may find himself on an emotional roller coaster and take you along for the ride.

I saw this hypersensitivity most clearly in parishioners facing divorce, especially those who had been rejected and were now being sued for divorce. The pain of their rejection is extreme. One of my parishioners lashed out at me for days after I talked with her husband and her about the divorce proceedings. She totally misconstrued what I had said and believed that I had verbally attacked her. Because as a pastor and professional I cannot "take sides" in disputes between members of my church, she never knew how much I sided with her and how strongly I believed her husband was behaving like a jerk.

In another case, one of my colleagues suffered the loss of her father. Julia and her brother cooperated well as they made arrangements for the funeral and settled the estate. The crisis came later, in a dispute over a small wooden cross.

In Julia's ethnic community, there is a custom of placing a small cross in the casket during viewing of the body. The cross is removed prior to burial and given to a surviving family member. As the eldest child, Julia, by custom, should have received the cross. But her younger brother requested it from the funeral director and has kept it. In her grief, Julia was deeply hurt and offended, and the succeeding estrangement between her brother and her has lasted nearly a decade.

If your loved one is feeling hypersensitive, simply stay near her and listen. In a crisis, a friend's role is to help the wounded lance and drain the poison from her emotions—an action requiring great love and patience.

*Loss.* At a recent dinner party I spoke with a woman whose two-year-old died accidently eighteen years ago. She continues to feel the void left in her life by that loss. She reflected what parents who have lost a child to death inevitably experience: "You never get over it."

The sense of loss is probably the longest-lived emotional response to a death. We err most when we fail to understand that our grieving friend will feel a sense of loss for the rest of her life.

I am shocked when friends and relatives decide that a grieving parent or widow has been "down" long enough. The concerns are often expressed blatantly. The mother of a teenager killed in an automobile accident is told, "Well, it's been six weeks now. It's time to dry the tears and get on with your life." Or a well-meaning Christian says to her, "You should rejoice because your son has gone to be with the Lord."

Balderdash! Such messages rarely end grief but often end relationships. In the face of such insensitivity, the bereaved quietly withdraws, fearing to show her emotions to people who cannot accept them. Her friends may have meant well when they said such things, but I'm afraid that they are simply protecting themselves from having to deal any longer with the continuing pain of the bereaved.

Of course some losses quickly wane. A teenager who loses her first boyfriend quickly forgets him when she falls in love with someone else. Or a family suffering from a financial crisis may be fine as soon as money flows again into the family economy.

Many losses are not reversible, however. The truly caring friend, committed for the long term, recognizes such loss, is present, and listens without offering any "quick fixes" for grief, whatever its cause. Spending time with a bereaved person, visiting, even distracting him or her from time to time with conversation, recreation, and entertainment, often help.

Over time, perhaps many years, the pain of loss will diminish so that your friend or relative can live creatively and happily, even though the void created by some losses is never completely filled. Your loving, caring, patient presence helps fill in some of the deepest holes.

*Abandonment.* Loss says: "My life feels so empty without you." Abandonment says: "I'll never forgive you for dying and leaving me alone." A sense of abandonment contains elements of loss and anger. Anger at the one who died? Yes, indeed. A rational conclusion? No, but emotional responses are, by definition, irrational. Grief itself is nonrational.

Frequently in my pastoral counseling, a widowed person asks, "Why did he die on me like this? Why did he leave me?" No matter that the deceased spouse died a long, painful death after a lengthy, valiant fight against a terminal disease. This feeling of abandonment is an honest, if irrational, expression of the survivor's grief.

There are times, however, when the feeling of abandonment is quite rational. If a husband leaves town with another woman, sues for divorce, and refuses to pay child support, his wife and children naturally feel abandoned. Or if a dedicated employee of thirty years is forced into retirement, he of course feels abandoned by the only company he has worked for his entire adult life. The family and friends of a person who committed suicide may feel abandoned, and so may an elderly parent when his children place him in a convalescent hospital.

As in various emotions and stages of grief, it is not for us to decide if an emotion makes sense. If a grieving person feels abandonment or any other emotional response, his feeling is as real and unavoidable as death and taxes. You waste your time and may even destroy your relationship if you try to talk a grieving friend out of his feelings. If his emotions are out of control, a professional counselor may be able to help. But the role of a friend is to listen, to be present, and to accept the emotions as they are.

*Anger.* In my experience anger is a component of everyone's grief—although it's sometimes expressed in unexpected ways.

Many of us have a problem accepting and expressing anger, so we learn to disguise it. The angriest person I know is also the drippiest, most saccharine person I know. Deanne's life is marked with losses, frustration, and disappointments, but her busyness and her syrupy talk keep her emotions and her loved ones at arm's length. Often her strained optimism exhausts her and those around her, for she rarely lets her guard down. The few times Deanne's sugar-coated veneer cracked in my presence were moments of great relief for her and me. Of course, her anger and hurt flooded out, almost overwhelming me. Yet those were our only moments of closeness, the only times her emotional responses felt appropriate. After each episode, however, Deanne quickly glossed over the crack in the veneer and fell back into her old way of life.

I've come to expect the bereaved to be angry, often angry at God (consider the book of Job and some of the psalms), often angry at the deceased loved one, frequently angry at a doctor or other professional conveniently nearby. Don't expect this anger to be rational or something you can intellectually resolve. Truly there is no justice in this life, and a person who is suffering great loss has a right to vocalize his or her grievance.

You, too, may be conveniently nearby. I admonish you once again: do not take your friend's negative words to heart. Clergy learn this early on. A close relative or intimate friend or trusted pastor may provide one of the safest relationships for the venting of one's emotions.

Young adults often express anger more openly. I've encountered some of my most difficult pastoral situations in gatherings of teenagers following a memorial service for a peer. These young people are also more open in their anger at the death of a parent or in response to their parents' divorce. Their anger in such cases is appropriate and understandable, yet it may surprise an adult friend who has never seen the young person have anything more than a casual, superficial attitude about life.

Your love is stronger than any destructive words. One of the greatest things you can do for a grieving friend is allow him to express his anger.

*Fear.* If there is an emotion we all can relate to regarding death and grief, it is fear. Most likely, our own response to the grief of another is fear: fear of their emotion and pain, fear that the loss they are suffering could be our own.

We fear the changeableness of life, our frailty and vulnerability. We wonder: "Will I survive in the face of this loss? Am I resourceful enough and strong enough to take care of myself and others who depend on me?"

I often counsel widows whose husbands had held the family's financial cards close to the vest. Suddenly the financial responsibility has been thrust upon these women without the experience or information they need to make good decisions, and they fear that they will bungle their finances.

Those grieving over a loss may become more possessive toward the people they love. This is most apparent when a child dies, and the parents fear losing their surviving children.

While teenagers faced with loss experience strong anger, younger children experience fear. Their fears may be allayed if their parents or other significant adults allow them to share in the grief process, ask questions, and seek reassurance.

An ageless truth says that our greatest fear is fear of the unknown. When a friend or loved one faces a great loss or change, an uncertain future makes fear inevitable.

The Bible says that "perfect love drives out fear" (1 John 4:18). While our love toward a friend or relative is far from perfect, it nonetheless reduces the anxiety of the grief-stricken one.

*Tears and hysterics.* Crying and hysterical outbursts were not on my original list of emotions associated with grief. I consider tears and hysteria expressions of one or more of the basic emotions. But a class of high school seniors, upon hearing the list, insisted I reconsider—they obviously prevailed.

The students argued that if this listing was to help them prepare for what to expect in grief and to help them ready themselves emotionally to face it, knowing how to face hysterical outbursts must be included. Quite simply, for them—and most likely all of us—it is a major challenge to comfort someone who is crying uncontrollably.

Tears are, of course, a natural release of feelings that might otherwise stay bottled up at the cost of physical or emotional health. Tears relieve pressures that otherwise translate into stress. Many people with chronic, stress-related ailments (which may include many forms of disease) never cry. Their hurt and pain then turns inward, poisoning them.

We would all be healthier if we could redefine for our culture what is an appropriate show of emotion. Some situations demand a stoic hold on our feelings, but there must also be times when we can release them. There is, as the Bible says, "a time to weep and a time to laugh" (Ecclesiastes 3:4).

Men are especially pressured into believing that tears are weak and feminine. Yet generally speaking, I have found women emotionally healthier and tougher than men. This is largely due to their ability to get feelings out, to cry without embarrassment and to move on in the grief process. Women spend more emotional energy meeting the demands of a crisis and less keeping the lid on. But culture pressures men to keep the lid on, when they would be better off if they would simply put their arms around their loved ones and sob.

When someone you love is crying, accept those tears not only as a healing force, but also as a display of love and trust. If your friend does not share her tears with you, however, don't press her. You should never manipulate such intimacy; manipulation violates trust. Take care not to trespass on the privacy of another, no matter how close you are.

**Guilt.** When someone special to us dies, feelings of remorse sweep across us. Recently a young friend and former parishioner of mine died thousands of miles away. After my initial shock and disbelief, I felt guilty—that I hadn't kept in touch better through the years, that I had never told him how important he was to me, that I was not there to help comfort his parents, sister, and friends.

I have felt guilt, though certainly not to the same degree, when revered public figures have died, especially due to tragic assassinations. Again, normal emotional responses in grief are often irrational.

The grief following the death of a relationship also is characterized by guilt in various forms. After a divorce, for instance, not only may each estranged spouse feel remorse; their young children will likely feel guilty and responsible for their parents' breakup. Even more heartrending is the deep guilt and shame felt by child victims of incest and abuse, who require intensive therapy to work through these emotions.

My father-in-law, Dr. John Kimball Saville, has observed in his pastoral work (now in its sixth decade) that grief is hardest not when family members have been close, but when a strained relationship leaves the survivor with unresolved guilt. In other words, your grandmother's grief will be difficult at the death of your grandfather after fifty-one years of happily married life. But your aunt (their daughter) will suffer more with guilt because of her forty-year rocky and estranged relationship with your grandfather, which she knows caused him much pain even in his final days.

Guilt can make the grief interminable. Parents who are responsible or believe themselves responsible for the accidental death of a child may torment themselves emotionally for decades. A close friend and parishioner lost his daughter from a playground fall which appeared minor at first. He told me that he should have been criminally prosecuted for her death. But no court anywhere would have found him guilty of anything nor punished him as much as he has punished himself through the years.

In every instance of guilt in grief, we always ask

ourselves the tormenting question: "What could I have done better or differently to prevent this loss?" A second question is even worse: "Why her, and not me?" Frequently such questions go unspoken, leaving the bereaved person with a general feeling of guilt without any apparent specific cause. Most of this passes in a few months. In instances of severe, sustained guilt, however, an individual may require professional help and years of healing.

**Depression.** Some emotional responses in grief are more obvious than others. Depression is one such condition. Any of us who have suffered any kind of loss have known depression. Experts in psychology and psychiatry tell us, in fact, that depression is the most common emotional illness of our day.

Earlier in this chapter I described the numbness that is often the first reaction in grief. The shock of traumatic loss is followed by denial and disbelief. Depression is a later response that comes as a result of accepting harsh reality. Depression may not prevent the afflicted person from responding to the demands of an emergency and providing for those depending on him, but depression will prevent him from moving ahead with his own life.

Depression is more than "the blues." It is an emotionally handicapping condition that renders life meaningless. The depressed person withdraws into herself, becoming listless and unresponsive. Heavy drinking, overeating, and other compulsive behaviors often signal a clinical depression. Often, these behaviors have already existed, but grief intensifies them.

Depressed friends often do not have the energy for conversation. Anything more than a question requiring a simple "yes" or "no" may pass by without an answer; the energy to respond simply isn't there. If you push your friend or loved one to "be happy," he may change his demeanor simply to get you to back off; it may require less emotional energy to give you the impression that he is better than to argue with you about his true feelings. Severely depressed persons require professional treatment to get well (see chapter 15).

A generation ago, Dr. Viktor Frankl, a psychiatrist who survived the Nazi death camps, developed a psychological approach to surviving the worst kind of suffering, loss, and depression. In his tremendous book, *Man's Search for Meaning*, he speaks of the meaning in life that enables us to survive.[2] One primary way a person finds meaning strong enough to beat depression is through love. Your patient love, your listening love, helps a loved one find a meaningful perspective on life that just may help pull her back from the edge.

*Withdrawal.* People in grief withdraw, at least for a while. Some withdrawal is due to depression, an emotional "battening down the hatches," which over time can develop into a serious condition. However, much withdrawal is appropriate, necessary, and understandable:

- Having been served with divorce papers earlier in the day, your business partner doesn't show for a dinner party in your home.

- Your child's godmother reneges on his seventh birthday party, her own little boy now comatose from an accident a few weeks earlier.

- A woman recently widowed decisively turns down your invitation to be a blind date for your uncle at a formal dinner.

In some cultures, relatives observe a set period of mourning the death of a family member. Properly honoring the dead includes withdrawal from many regular activities in favor of quiet family gatherings and religious observances. Such a period also honors the grief process, allowing time to work through the kinds of emotional responses we consider here.

Further, a person in the midst of a personal crisis or loss may be overwhelmed by tasks and responsibilities thrust upon her. For instance, a young widow may not only have emergency legal and financial details to address and a funeral to plan but children to care for in their grief—all of which take precedence over her personal grief.

In the months following a loss, a grieving friend may withdraw from relationships because, tragically, friends and relatives have withdrawn from her. Not knowing what to say or do, they neither communicate nor help; out of a sense of helplessness and embarrassment, they have withdrawn.

The caring friend strikes a balance between giving the bereaved time and not letting the friendship slip away. Honor your friend's privacy and need to withdraw, but never withhold sincere offers of help or invitations to get together.

*Exhaustion.* A grieving person is an exhausted person. Emotional exhaustion also may account for your friend's withdrawal from you and others. He may simply have no psychic energy left for you or anyone or anything else.

There is no tiredness like emotional exhaustion. If you are physically tired, you will probably sleep well; one or two nights of good rest will probably refresh and renew you. Not so with emotional tiredness. You may not feel truly rested until the underlying emotional stress gradually eases.

Rudy, a close friend, faced a marital crisis. His wife wanted a divorce, and he spent every measure of energy trying to work out a reconciliation. He was neither sleeping well at night nor staying fully awake during the day. Another friend of Rudy's was miffed at his preoccupation. He felt neglected and thought Rudy was being selfish. This friend was insensitive to Rudy's pain and the amount of emotional energy required to deal with a potential loss. Happily, my friend and his wife reconciled over time. He began sleeping well at night and immediately resumed his demanding daytime professional schedule. I have enjoyed continued friendship with Rudy and his wife. But his relationship with less patient friends may never be the same again.

Your understanding of your friend's exhaustion tempers your expectations of his involvement with life and relationships. Every practical chore you can perform for someone whose energy is already stretched to the limit is important.

**Physical Symptoms.** Until recently, this list of emotional responses to grief contained seventeen categories. Then I conducted a workshop in a California church where lay ministries assistant Jean Smith spoke of physical symptoms she suffered as a result of emotional stress following her husband's death. A number of other widows in the group concurred, telling of such ailments as hoarseness and back pain, all of which lessened as their grief eased.

Medical experts also have noted that prolonged emotional stress causes physical health problems. For decades psychiatrists have observed psychosomatic illnesses—real physical ailments brought on by psychological causes.

To repeat: these are *real* physical conditions regardless of their cause. Whenever someone becomes physically ill during or after a crisis, I urge him or her to see a physician. Following the death of my father, I was very concerned about my mother's physical condition and fussed at her until she saw her doctor.

**Doubts and Spiritual Crises.** I know a number of people, including clergy, who believe that no one with deep religious faith need ever face a spiritual crisis due to loss. Indeed, some would argue that none of the emotional responses to grief listed in this chapter should affect the "true believer." It is as though they believe the faithful no longer feel human emotions—or shouldn't.

In counseling people, however, I have come to expect doubt and pained questioning as a part of grief. In pastoring people, I have come to welcome emotions associated with grief as a part of faith development. In studying the Scriptures, I have come to realize that human emotions and their appropriate release are a part of God's created order; even Jesus wept at the death of a friend (John 11:35) and despaired in a moment of agony (Mark 15:34).

When a friend or loved one talks about faith that has been shaken—faith in God, faith in other people, faith in himself—take a deep breath and listen. Your love and attentiveness will help steady his confidence. Encourage him to talk over spiritual concerns with a trusted clergyperson. Don't be frightened away when a bereaved friend expresses the doubts and spiritual loneliness that so often accompany grief.

*Resignation or Acceptance.* In her work with the dying, Dr. Elisabeth Kubler-Ross noted that the final emotional stage for many of her patients was acceptance of death.[3] Over time we can expect most grieving people to progress to accepting death. Time is the key—lots of time—in many cases, years. While a friend or loved one will never forget the tragic death of a child or a bitter divorce, she may come to accept it and go on to fully and creatively engage in life. I've witnessed it in countless situations. We may never get over our grief, but we can get better.

By resignation I mean fully facing the reality of loss and of the need to proceed with life with less than complete emotional healing. For instance, the wife of a thirty-year-old man dying of cancer resigns herself to her coming loss, takes charge of her husband's treatment and business affairs, makes preliminary funeral arrangements, and takes over the full parenting responsibility for their four sons. She has resigned herself to her husband's death. Accepting the death of her beloved, however, may be a long way off.

Resignation and acceptance are listed here so that you can recognize these responses when you encounter them. However, a caring friend should not try to push the bereaved into resignation and then to acceptance. Acceptance may well signal the completion of the grief process.

*Relief.* A middle-aged friend of mine devoted eight years to the care of her invalid father. After each increasingly serious hospitalization, Beth Ann brought him back to her home. She honored his strong feelings against hospitals and his final wish to die at home in his own bed. In the final weeks a respirator pumped oxygen into his lungs and forced it out, intravenous tubes dripped painkillers into his bloodstream, and a tube through his nose supplied nutrients directly into his stomach. One day he died peacefully in a deep coma, his beloved daughter at his bedside.

Soon after Beth Ann took care of the last needs of her father's physical being, she felt overwhelming relief, first for him, then for herself. She then fell into a deep and restful sleep.

In the middle of the night, Beth Ann awoke. Although her father was gone, she automatically hurried to his bedroom. She knew in her head that he was finally released from pain and now at peace, but in her heart she would know a profound sense of loss for the next two years. When we lose a parent, we lose one who has occupied the world with us since we breathed our first. Also, she had increasingly built her life around him and his care all those years; now she was faced with finding another central occupation, vocation, and even meaning to her life.

Beth Ann's relief also triggered guilt. In caring for her father, she had suffered immensely, both emotionally and financially. But after he was gone, she felt guilty for being relieved that she didn't have to struggle so hard anymore. Intellectually she is assured that not a cent was spared for his comfort and care; yet she feels selfish and guilty.

I have observed and stood by many friends and parishioners in similar experiences. As medical technology prolongs our lives, more and more of us will struggle with the many issues and emotions surrounding the life support of a loved one.

Even more poignant is the response of loved ones to the suicide of a family member. Clay died in his thirties from a drug overdose. For twenty years he had been a financial and emotional burden to his parents. When he died, his parents felt a deep sense of failure. Yet they were also overwhelmed with relief that the hell he had created for himself and for all who cared about him was no more.

As I wrote earlier, grief is often a complex of emotions that appear to contradict each other. Indeed, the human mind is filled with apparently contradictory emotional responses. The role of a caring friend or relative is to respect and accept such responses.

**Mental Illness.** Occasionally a person cannot deal with the emotions of grief and develops significant psychological disability. I have had occasion to refer grieving people to mental health professionals, although I don't consider everyone I've referred to be mentally ill.

I can think of very few grieving people who required hospitalization. Yet from my reading I know that a large percentage of people in mental health facilities are there because of an inadequate response to grief—some estimates average around thirty percent.

Most of us survive any number of emotionally stressful losses in a lifetime with little professional assistance. Having close and caring relatives and friends is probably the best preventive medicine for any number of emotional ailments. Some situations, however, are "over the heads" of caring friends. Should you learn of any threat of suicide or other desperate action, for instance, or if your friend appears to be incoherent, you should find him professional help rather than attempting to care for him on your own.

## A PRECIOUS GIFT

Recognizing and understanding the emotional responses of grief help you respond more effectively to your grieving friend. If you have developed a trusting friendship, one that permits your friend to share the deepest feelings of her heart, you have given her a rare and precious gift. May each of us know such a friend. May each of us become one.

# — 6 —

# Know Available Resources

Over ten years ago, the clergy leaders of Beverly Hills tried without much success to develop a Meals on Wheels program for shut-ins. After some research we discovered a group of senior citizens who were trying to establish a similar program. Once we joined forces, brought in the city government, the hospital, and various professionals willing to give their time and expertise to the project, we were awesome! Beverly Hills Meals on Wheels has flourished ever since. Our love and respect for each other has also flourished as we united to serve the needs of our neighbors.

As you care for a hurting relative, don't isolate yourself or your relative from the wide array of resources available to assist you both. You, too, will discover persons and organizations of good will, commitment, and expertise. With their help, you will be awesome, too.

## Build on Your Caring Abilities

You already have caring impulses and talents. You already have the desire to develop them further. I know these things about you because you have chosen to read a book on caring.

Experience is your teacher as you develop your ability to care. Reading, taking classes, and training as a volunteer can help you learn more about caring for others in all sorts of situations.

*Reading.* When I teach students caring skills, I assign the following books: *The Friendship Factor* by Alan Loy McGinnis,[1] a general introduction to loving relationships; *On Death and Dying* by Elisabeth Kubler-Ross,[2] her classic work on emotions surrounding death; and *Twelve Steps and Twelve Traditions of Alcoholics Anonymous,*[3] a therapeutic method used by many support groups for various addictions and problems. Dr. Leo Buscaglia's books on loving also provide helpful teaching on caring.[4]

When I select books, articles, and pamphlets, I act on a recommendation of a friend or colleague whose judgment I trust, or the recommendation of the author's credentials and experience. If the material is recommended by an expert or an organization known for work in the field, I feel confident about what I read. Most of the organizations listed in the Appendix produce excellent publications in their area of concern. Also, be alert for audiotapes and videotapes on pertinent topics.

*Classes.* From introductory psychology courses in your local community college to higher-level classes offered by a university, there are many opportunities for you to study inexpensively, conveniently, and close to home.

When I browsed through the schedules of various schools in my area, I found Saturday workshops on relationships at an adult school; introductory courses in personality development at the community college; and a class in gerontology (understanding the aging) at the university. I also have advertisements from medical centers, one providing a free workshop on chemical dependency, the other announcing a course on troubled adolescents. Sometimes churches or schools offer lectures on specific topics.

You do not need to take a formal class in order to become a caring person. But for many of us, taking a formal class increases our confidence and decreases our fear of dealing with a hurting relative.

**Volunteering.** You may discover through helping those close to you that you want to do more for people in crisis situations. The best volunteer programs give you both the training you need and the opportunity to provide meaningful, effective service.

One of the high school seniors in my class on caring became a counselor on a teen suicide hot line. To prepare for such important peer counseling, he successfully completed an extensive training program taught by mental health professionals.

Another student took the training to become an "AIDS Buddy," a volunteer assigned to assist persons suffering with AIDS. Most of her training applies to working with anyone with a terminal illness.

The most complete and comprehensive volunteer training I know is part of the national "Stephen Ministry" program offered by many local congregations. The program prepares church members as peer pastoral counselors. Initial training, which lasts for nearly a year, must be completed before actual contacts with fellow members of the congregation are permitted. Training then continues as long as the volunteer participates in the program.

Various kinds of institutions that care for people need volunteers. Virtually every hospital relies on its volunteer force to function, and hospices train their volunteers to work with the dying. Volunteering provides a wonderful opportunity to share and develop your caring abilities.

## Where to Turn for Help

Effectiveness in any job includes a keen awareness of one's own limitations—knowing when to seek help and where to get it. The kind of pastoral counseling I do consists largely in active listening. I provide support, act as a release valve, and help to clarify the counselee's own feelings and options. Only rarely do I tell a counselee what he should do. In your role as a caring friend, you can provide the same kind of help by your presence, by listening, and by offering support.

Through training and experience I am also able to diagnose deeper problems and to refer a counselee for professional assistance beyond pastoral counseling. I also know resources in the larger community for further information and guidance. As a caring friend, you will sometimes need to do the same.

**Professionals.** Most Americans first turn to their family doctor or clergyperson in times of emotionally wrenching crisis or loss. Astute physicians and clergy know the kinds of symptoms that call for counseling. They maintain a list of qualified therapists and match the person to the appropriate specialist. If you are unsure how to help a loved one in crisis, check with your doctor or pastor first.

Usually, I refer counselees to one of three kinds of mental health professionals licensed by the state to provide therapy: a psychiatrist, a medical doctor who can administer drugs and hospitalize patients, as well as do counseling; a licensed psychologist (with a doctorate in psychology); or a Marriage, Family, and Child Counselor (M.F.C.C.), who performs psychotherapy as well.

Other options for counseling include specialized nurses and clinical social workers. Clinics and community counseling centers staffed by teams of various types of professionals see clients as needed through the progress of their therapy. Many churches also have counseling centers. Finally, there are centers for drug rehabilitation and eating disorders.

Selecting a counselor, like choosing a doctor or lawyer, is critical. Often a person's philosophy, goals, personality, and experience matter as much as her degrees. To find a qualified therapist, get recommendations from people you trust, and check for qualifications. Then go for an initial interview before committing yourself or your friend to a long-term counseling relationship. If after a time you find that your needs are not being met, do not hesitate to find another counselor.

*Support Groups.* Alcoholics Anonymous was the first group organized for the mutual support of troubled people. Not only has A.A. spread around the world, it has given birth: first to its Alanon and Alateen family support programs, then to dozens of other support groups, such as Gamblers Anonymous, Overeaters Anonymous, and Narcotics Anonymous. In addition to these national groups, many community organizations, churches, and synagogues also tailor groups to meet special needs. A congregation in my area, for example, provides a support group for parents of handicapped children.

How do you locate these groups in your own community? Many phone books list community services at the front, including crisis hot lines, organizations, and support groups. In the yellow pages look under headings like "Social Service Organizations," or "Women's Organizations and Services," "Support Groups," or "Alcohol Information and Treatment Centers." Local newspapers sometimes carry listings of support groups. In a Boulder, Colorado, newspaper I found eighty support groups listed, from "Adult Stuttering Support Group" to "Women's Recovery Center." You can also contact local support groups through most of the national organizations listed in the Appendix. The National Center for Health Information will provide you with the telephone number of a support group clearinghouse in your state. Their address and phone number is listed at the end of the Appendix.

**Organizations.** The Appendix lists organizations that assist persons in crisis and those who care about them. Many organizations have an 800-number. Although most of them respond without charge, I urge you to give a contribution to defray their costs and to further their work.

# PART III

# Responding to Crisis and Loss

# — 7 —

# At a Time of Death

I still remember the night my great-grandmother died. I was barely four years old, and nearly four decades have passed. Yet many details remain imprinted on my memory: how she looked, the tall oxygen tank at her bedside in my great-aunt's home, my mother's and aunt's tears, the cold night air in the driveway, the arrival of the ambulance, the fear and confusion I felt when my mother told me of her death. That is my first memory of someone dying.

A few years later, an uncle on my father's side died after a lingering illness. I can still picture him in his hospital bed and, a few days later, lying in his casket. I remember my fear at the extreme grief of my grandmother and my aunts.

I was sixteen when my grandfather died, the first death of a close family member. Of course, I recall almost every detail of his final days and funeral. I felt most of the emotional responses to grief discussed in this book.

The memories of a person's encounters with death and the accompanying emotions significantly affect that person's ability to respond to others when they are facing the death of a loved one. Usually these memories and emotions create empathy with grieving friends, reminding us of what we can do to ease their pain. But sometimes these memories can cause such pain that they hinder us from reaching out to a hurting friend. If you find that observing a loved one's grief resurrects your own pain from unresolved losses in your life, you may want to seek counseling. Likely, such grief is inhibiting many of your relationships.

## Your Initial Response

In addition to being aware of your own feelings as you enter into the grief of your friend, review these suggestions for your initial response.

*Be in contact.* Respond early on (see chapter 2 for a detailed discussion of helpful responses). Call, visit, write—do something—*as soon as* you learn of the death of someone close to your friend or loved one. You may argue that you should put off personal contact until it seems "more appropriate" so that you won't "disturb" your friend—but she is already "disturbed." Putting off your first contact with her only makes it embarrassing when you contact her too late—or worse, it may damage your relationship. If the time is not right for a visit, your friend will tell you, either verbally or nonverbally.

Make contact and stay in touch. Even more important than your actions is the unspoken message that you care, that you are standing by; such messages keep friendship and love alive even in the most trying times.

From your first communication, don't be afraid to talk about the person who died. Talk about what he meant to you, and talk about what he meant to your friend. You may say things like, "I always appreciated his dry sense of humor," or "You must really miss your dad; I know how much you loved him."

**Let your friend talk.** Don't be afraid to allow the bereaved person to talk about the one who died. Beware of changing the subject or freezing up when the name of the deceased is mentioned. A friend of mine who lost her young brother in a tragic accident and who knew I was addressing this subject said: "Tell them to let us talk about our loved one who died." That was her number-one admonition to family and friends who care about the bereaved. Listening is not only therapeutic for your friend, listening deepens your relationship with your friend (see chapter 4).

**Expect emotional crises.** Prepare for an emotional roller-coaster ride (see chapter 5). Grief differs even as emotional makeup differs from individual to individual. Don't anticipate the feelings of your friend or attempt to orchestrate his responses. His own personality and situation determines what emotions he feels, in what order they confront him, in what time frame they come and go, and in front of whom he is willing to be vulnerable to various emotions.

## Immediate Concerns of the Family
## of One Who Has Died

Rarely is a family less prepared to make decisions, conduct business, and advocate their interests than when a loved one dies. Yet death creates a situation when many such issues must be resolved. They are briefly discussed here to give you an idea of what your friends are going through, or so that if they ask, you can make this part of the journey with them.

*Legal procedures* may begin with waiting for a death certificate. Certification of the cause of death is prescribed by state law and is often the responsibility of the county coroner. If a person dies in a hospital, a doctor usually signs the death certificate. Once the death certificate has been signed, the body is released to the family for burial.

If the person dies accidentally, at home, or in some other circumstance not certifiable by a personal physician, the coroner will likely take custody of the body to determine the cause of death. There may be a police investigation or even an autopsy and tissue studies, which may require weeks. Occasionally, especially in larger metropolitan counties, a bureaucratic delay may keep the coroner from releasing the body to a mortuary.

Each step of this procedure increases the trauma of the family already suffering the unexpected death of a member. In some cases, the cause of death is never determined, which can complicate grief and cloud the circumstances of the death. I have seen unanswered questions torture parents after the sudden death of a child either by accident or unexplained natural causes.

**Medical decisions** often accompany the death of a loved one. Family members may have to deal with paramedics, emergency room personnel, or doctors. They may be subjected to intense questioning and reams of paperwork. Or they may have to decide when to remove life-support systems from their loved one.

After a death the family may need to decide whether to allow an autopsy for medical research purposes. They may be asked to allow organ or tissue donation. Some families readily permit these procedures, while others feel pressured and confused. I have known family members who feel their loved one endured too much medical intervention in the last days and emotionally reject any further procedure, especially an autopsy.

**Spiritual issues** to attend to vary according to personal need and religious belief. Some families request that their loved one receive last rites, while others simply request the presence of their pastor at the time of death. Most families will want to contact a pastor and arrange memorial services. You might offer to initiate contact with their pastor.

**Mortuary arrangements** begin with deciding which funeral home to deal with. Once that decision is made, the mortuary will come to the house, hospital, or county morgue for the body. Early on, the family meets with a funeral director to gather information for documents, permits, and certificates; to decide on preparation and disposition of the body; to purchase a burial place or arrange for scattering of ashes; to make preliminary arrangements for memorial services; to determine costs. Sometimes the deceased person may have prearranged all of these details.

If the body is to be viewed, the funeral director asks the family to bring the person's favorite dressy suit of clothes and a good color photograph to help the cosmetologist achieve the individual's natural skin tones.

Discussions about the body may be emotional; certainly viewing the body will elicit great feeling. Few experiences confront a loved one with the finality of death more than the lifeless body of the beloved. Such confrontation is a necessary step for the family to accept the death and begin to grieve. Think twice before "protecting" anyone, even a child, from facing this reality.

### Memorial Services and Other Gatherings

I believe gatherings of family and friends in the name of one who has died are critically important for those who are left behind. Even when the deceased person did not want to have a funeral service, I encourage those who have been left behind to have one if it will help them. In my religious tradition, such services are for the survivors, not the deceased, who is safely in the arms of God. I urge survivors to do what they need to do to rally the loving support of their friends, family, and church.

Memorial services are important for several reasons. First, they give us an opportunity to celebrate the life of the person who has died. Second, they enable us to release the loved one and commit him or her to God's eternal protection and care. Third, they help us to comfort each other. Fourth, they give us a chance to remind ourselves of the great truths and promises of our faith. Last, they help us make peace in our hearts with the death of the loved one—and with death itself.

*The traditional funeral* in the United States usually includes: (1) viewing the body a day or so before burial, often with a brief religious service the night before; (2) a service in a funeral home or church with the body present; and (3) a brief service at the grave. Relatives and friends are traditionally invited to all these gatherings, although in recent years one or more may be private, reserved for only the closest family members.

*Cremation* has become a widely accepted practice in recent years and is permitted in many major religious groups. I would estimate that fifty percent of my parishioners in the last decade have favored immediate cremation followed by a memorial service. The ashes are often scattered (at sea or in a garden) or buried with or without the family present, with or without a religious service.

*Gatherings or "wakes"* following burial or memorial services provide helpful opportunities for fellowship, mutual support, and emotional catharsis. You may help provide food or coordinate the event or, in certain situations, even make your home available for the gathering.

In my church we tried to be "family" to older members of the congregation who had no relatives nearby. Often, after the death of one of our dear "senior saints," we opened the church to a gathering, and a church member also opened her home to mourners.

This past year a close family friend suffered the death of his father. Dave made hurried arrangements for the funeral, deciding that he wanted as little fuss and emotion as possible. In fact, we almost did not find out about his loss—for he didn't tell us—and we barely made it to the memorial service. Although Dave hadn't wanted a large gathering, he was overwhelmed by the love and support he and his family received from the many friends who love them. His attitude about funerals was transformed. He now appreciates the support of "outside" folks for "inside" hurts and losses, and he relishes gatherings of family and friends.

Share as fully as you can in the services and gatherings following a loss to someone close to you. It is one of the greatest gifts of friendship and caring you can give.

## Practical Helps

When someone dies, some special needs may arise in the following five categories.

*Communication.* Obviously the death of a member severely alters the routine of a household. Appointments and schedules must be changed. Arrangements must be made. Perhaps you can offer to cover the telephone, which may be ringing off the hook once news of the death gets around. You may also be able to help with letters and forms.

There is also the necessary task of notifying others of the death and the family's plans and desires. Close relatives should be informed immediately. Other calls, however, should wait until memorial service arrangements and other information can be shared in the same call, thus preventing the need for more than one round of telephoning. The funeral home helps the family prepare a notice for the newspaper.

*Transportation.* You and your car may be of major assistance to friends dealing with the death of a loved one. You may help them get to appointments, get children to and from school, run errands, or shuttle relatives to and from the airport, train station, or bus depot.

*Domestic duties.* Many household routines must be carried on, regardless of the crisis and its pain, especially if there are young children or other dependent persons. There may be numerous visitors and even house guests to prepare for and attend to. Perhaps you can offer to baby-sit, help with household chores, or organize a group of friends to bring in meals.

*Hospitality.* Following a death, survivors have no time or inclination to prepare meals. In addition, they may have guests to feed, or they may need to provide a buffet for a gathering of mourners. You could offer to cook a meal, coordinate a buffet, or make arrangements for meals to be brought in.

In addition to food, the family may need help with its many visitors. You could offer to greet and attend to callers, who may be numerous. Or you could open your home to out-of-town relatives who need a place to stay.

*Professional services.* You may have professional skills or knowledge to offer a family suffering the death of a loved one. In my parish ministry, for instance, we were blessed with attorneys who volunteered to assist indigent members of the church family at such times. If you offer professional help, make sure that it does not present a conflict of interest, and do not push your way into the situation or take on decisions and responsibilities that belong to the survivor.

## The Nature of Grief Following a Death

In chapters 4 and 5 I discussed the emotions of grief and how you can help your friend by listening. In addition to the material in those chapters, knowing the following specific characteristics of the grief process following the death of a loved one will equip you to effectively help a friend.

*Expect a lengthy process,* measured more likely in years than in days. Friends and relatives commonly—and grossly—underestimate the time required for the grief process. I'm sure it is a manifestation of our culture's and our own denial of death; our philosophy seems to be "don't talk about it, and maybe it will go away." To attempt to speed up bereavement is not only folly but can also become the cause of severe strain on your relationship. Be patient.

*Be aware of factors that intensify grief.* I find three to be particularly pertinent. First, a sudden and unexpected death causes more intense grief than if the death was expected for a long time. Second, a violent and painful death creates more severe grief than a peaceful death of natural causes. Third, the untimely death of a younger person causes more intense pain than the timely death of one who has led a full life. For example, the violent suicide of a teenager would, quite naturally, evoke a stronger response than the death of an eighty-year-old grandfather.

## Your Response in the Long Term

Because your friend or relative's grief may last a long time, you will need to support her in the months following the death as intensely as you did initially. Often throngs of people surround the bereaved at first, but most of them won't keep in touch after a few days. Blessed are those few friends and relatives who continue their regular calls, visits, and invitations over the long haul.

Keeping in touch is a significant expression of caring in the long term. Your relationship will grow in the process. One of our closest family friendships is with the widow of a community leader; what had been a close comradeship between two men has evolved into a close relationship that includes wives and children. Take the initiative to keep in touch, and respond to invitations from your friend.

Remembering holidays and other "together" times is also important. For many years ahead such occasions as Christmas, birthdays, and anniversaries will likely trigger emotional moments, provoking happy memories as well as sad longings. Time is a healer, true; but time also sets emotional traps on significant dates throughout the year. Your role as a caring comrade is not to remind a friend of such occasions but to stay close enough in communication that you can lovingly respond when needed. Perhaps you can include your friend in your own celebrations of holidays and other observances you share in common.

## Some Thoughts About Widowhood

I have observed that our culture predisposes us to act in certain ways toward widowed persons. Most of my observations come from ministering to women in their retirement years who have lost their husbands after long marriages; I'm sure they represent the majority of widowed women. Much of what I find to be cruel and unjust for such widows seems to be improving, largely perhaps as other women's issues are addressed.

Many women are regarded by society as attachments to or extensions of their husbands, and they are treated by many as nonentities once their husbands are gone. Some organizations drop them from membership following the death of the husband. Long-standing groups of couples to which the woman and her husband belonged may likewise drop her, as will many other friends who only knew her as part of a pair. Some of this may be the unintentional behavior of friends who cannot face death and the emotions of grief, but some of it is quite intentional, written into country club rules.

*Include the widowed friend* as you would have when he or she was married. Encourage others in your mutual circle of friends to do the same.

*Be sensitive to particularly lonely times.* In addition to days with special meaning (holidays, birthdays, anniversaries), my widowed friends tell me that early evenings and Sunday afternoons, times when a couple might slow down the pace enough to connect with each other, are especially difficult. You might find out about other lonely times for your friend, when a telephone call or little visit might be especially helpful. Even brief contact at the right moment can improve an entire day.

**Be attentive.** Respect your widowed friend as an individual. You may be pleasantly surprised to discover a person you've never really known before. Take the time to get acquainted.

**Don't be overattentive,** especially in trying to run your friend's life. Respect is the watchword here, too. Don't push her into personal decisions or into romantic relationships; such pushiness manifests our cultural discomfort with widowhood and death.

Your love and patience toward one who has lost a family member cannot fill the great void created by that death, but you can help immeasurably by listening, by standing with her or him, and by caring for specific needs.

# 8

# *At the Death of a Child*

Tommy died of cystic fibrosis at the age of seven. He was my parishioner and my friend. I still remember him standing at the edge of the church patio where we "checked in" with each other each Sunday after I had greeted the congregation. I would turn around, and there he would be. Sometimes we discussed a point of theology; sometimes I teased him about his favorite rock and roll group (whose music I never understood).

Tommy's parents first brought him to our church because of our reputation as a caring community that valued children's education. But I learned far more from Tommy than we could have imparted to him. With his parents, he drove home the lesson that the quality of life is far more important than the quantity of years. That little family packed more into those seven precious years than most of us will in our lifetime. They made every day count. They treasured their hours and days together. When I first met Tommy, the life expectancy for children with cystic fibrosis was the late teens or early twenties. I would have never believed that we would have even less time.

Tommy was intelligent; but even more, he was wise. As do many terminally ill persons, Tommy cared for his loved ones even as they cared for him. His last night on earth, ironically the night of the annual telethon for cystic fibrosis, he phoned in two pledges from his hospital room, vehemently proclaiming to his parents, as they kept watch at his bedside, that his disease was conquerable and that he would beat the statistics. He died in his mother's arms, a few days shy of his eighth birthday.

The night before his funeral, I arrived early at the funeral home. I wanted some time to see him alone, to face my own grief before trying to steel myself to help the others. The kind and understanding mortician greeted me, and we stood together looking at Tommy's body. I had built up my emotional defenses over the years to the point that I would cry only in response to touching scenes in films, where I could relax in the privacy of a darkened theater. But no amount of "professionalism" nor years of pastoral experience could defend me from the pain of that moment. I cried.

The evening at the funeral home went beautifully, as did every aspect of the services for Tommy. Of course, we held each other and held each other up. The children in attendance did fine, as children usually do; they were allowed to express their curiosity and ask their questions as they viewed their little friend's body.

Tommy, who had helped us all face his disease in

life, even helped us that night. A lover of details and gadgets, Tommy had owned a large watch with interesting functions and sound effects, including a whole system of preset alarms. His parents had strapped that watch on his wrist before the viewing. Every now and then, a loud *beep* sounded from inside the casket. Once, an unsuspecting mortician standing nearby jumped. The children and I all giggled.

At the funeral the following morning, hundreds (half of them children) gathered for a beautiful celebration of Tommy's life. In my homily I pledged our commitment to fight diseases that kill children, even as Tommy had fought his. Relieved to make it through the service with my emotions in check, I stood alongside Tommy's casket, closed for the burial service, as everyone who had attended passed by.

The last group to exit were his close friends from Cub Scouts in their blue uniforms. As they stood reverently in tribute to the comrade they would never laugh and run with again, the tragedy and injustice of it all washed over me. Stepping aside for a few moments, I wept. In those few moments, my humanity came fully alive. I changed that day, and I have liked the change in me ever since.

The committal service at the cemetery was short and special. I have returned many times to that spot, sometimes to mark a special day with Tommy's family, sometimes for myself. The gathering in his family home following the memorial service was also touching and memorable. Many of us became closer friends and better people because we knew Tommy.

In some ways I am surprised that I recall so many

details of Tommy's story. But then, I remember much about each child and young adult whose untimely, tragic, and unjust deaths I have confronted in my pastoral work. I continue to be very close to many of their families, united by a powerful bond of love, experience, and memories.

Reviewing the information about the death of a loved one (chapter 7) and the emotions of grief (chapter 5) can help you respond sensitively to a family who has lost a child. Yet you will need to know more about this loss and how to respond in the short and long term.

## The Nature of the Loss

Few family experiences are more devastating and tragic than the death of a child. The grief I have observed in parents whose child has died is nearly incomprehensible, unfathomable, and unending. They experience all the powerful emotions of grief, but with even greater intensity. Their anger and guilt can become all-consuming, even destructive.

*The age of the child* is, in some ways, irrelevant. Deep inside us, we believe that our children will outlive us, and it seems a violation of nature when a child dies before his parents. A retirement-age friend of mine continues to be in extreme pain from the violent death of his adult son six years ago; the love of his wife, other children, grandchildren, and countless friends has only slightly eased his pain.

In recent years mental health professionals have recognized the grief of parents who have lost the youngest of all children, the stillborn. Previously, they assumed that mothers of stillborn babies or babies who survived only a few hours after birth would not grieve like mothers who had raised a child for five or ten or fifteen years. That reasoning was totally incorrect; the grief of these parents is quite severe. The heartbreak of a parent whose child has died is not determined by the age of the child. To a parent, such a loss is always untimely.

***The siblings of the child who died*** must deal with their own grief as well as the reactions of their parents, often with far-reaching effects. The age of a sibling, of course, largely determines how her own grief will proceed and how she will react to the needs of her parents. I have known families that either cling to surviving children for fear of losing them, subtly push siblings into the footsteps of the deceased child, or neglect and ignore the surviving sibling in favor of honoring the one who died.

Often as harmful to children as the death itself is when their parents' respond poorly to the death. At least half of the couples who suffer the death of a child experience long-lasting emotional or marital problems that spill over onto the surviving children. A child's whole world is out of kilter when a parent is emotionally ill or the family is disintegrating.

***The marriage relationship*** must absorb a great deal of shock when a child dies. Whatever strains on the marriage existed before such a loss will be intensified in this tragedy.

The guilt of many bereaved parents can be all-consuming. If one parent feels responsible for the death of a child, the other may not only allow the spouse to feel that way, but also heap blame on the other, doubling the burden. Anger, too, will be understandably strong. It can be a deadly weapon in the hands of a grieving spouse who is looking to pick a fight.

*A very lengthy process of grief* is normal for parents who have lost a child. In some ways, few, if any, parents ever get over the loss.

In the parishes I've served, I've come to know many parents of soldiers who died in Vietnam. The mothers, typically, gave service, support, and leadership to the congregation. They regularly attended worship services and were upheld by the spiritual life of the congregation.

In contrast, the fathers who had lost sons in Vietnam were totally withdrawn from and antagonistic toward the church and God. I thought that the husbands were burned out by overwork in the parish, were abused in some way by a church leader early in life, or were calculated atheists blaming the church for every ill in human history. I discovered, instead, that each father had been happily active in church until a moment of overwhelming loss: the death of a son, in many cases an only son, in the Vietnam War. Now these fathers, in deep rage and hurt, were refusing to forgive God for the deaths of their sons.

I remember only one major breakthrough among these parents. On a visit to Washington, D.C., I made a pilgrimage to the Vietnam Memorial. Upon my return to California I called the parents of some of the soldiers whose names I'd seen on the black marble of the

Memorial. I remember in detail the moving conversations I had, speaking to both father and mother on extension telephones, sharing our emotions and our grief. That evening I made connections as significant to me as my visit to the Memorial. I do not know if the estranged fathers ever returned to their faith or their church, but I know that I at least was somehow able to be with them in their bereavement.

Still, their grief lives on. From the little contact I've had with these parents recently, I know that now, two decades since they lost their sons in Vietnam, their sorrow continues.

## Appropriate Responses to Bereaved Parents

If the loss of a child is immeasurable, so also is the significance of the loving support of relatives and friends. While none of us can ever fill the void left by such a tragic death, we can help—immeasurably. Keeping in mind the potential good you can do may encourage you to respond to such a painful tragedy.

I opened this book with the story of my first encounter with the death of a young child. A novice in the area of grief, I was hesitant to get involved. Even after that experience, I often still feel hesitant and fearful when making the first contact with parents following the death of a little one. I have taken long, deep breaths while staring at the telephone. I have sat in my car for long minutes before approaching the front door. I may forget to pray at other times, but I've never forgotten to pray for strength and guidance at those moments.

Probably no amount of training or experience will

remove the anxiety you feel about visiting grieving parents. Understandably, such situations will be difficult for you personally, and you may seek all sorts of ways to avoid them. But remember, you have the potential to be of real support.

As you stand by the grieving parents, you may need to seek support yourself from others you can talk to. And don't be surprised at how sensitive and sympathetic the bereaved family may be toward you. Many persons exhibit a special grace even in the midst of devastating circumstances.

The approach to reaching out to the bereaved described in chapter 7 also applies to families that lose a child; but in every respect, expect the experience of losing a child to be more intense and respond accordingly. The following three responses, effective in other situations of grief, can help sustain friends during the loss of a child as well.

*First, be present.* If you are a relative or close friend and your presence seems appreciated, stay with the bereaved as much as you can. I have occasionally found it helpful to stay with a family until they are too tired to stay awake any longer, even until they've gently suggested I leave. A family with no other close relatives or friends nearby especially appreciates your company. (See chapter 3.)

*Second, let them talk about the child who died.* When we avoid mentioning the name of the deceased child or find ways to cut off references to her by family members, we are most likely protecting ourselves rather than helping the bereaved. It is essential that a mourning parent or other loved one talk about the child who died. When professionals counsel grieving patients, they spend much of their time drawing out the patient's memories and feelings about the deceased loved one. Such conversation is healthy and therapeutic. (See chapter 4.)

*Third, expect a lengthy process of grieving.* The time required for the grief process is more realistically measured in years rather than weeks or months. It is not unusual for parents to grieve the death of a child for the remainder of their lives. The pain of loss will probably get worse before it gets better in the year following the death, will likely diminish over the longer term, yet may never totally go away. (See chapter 5.)

Your role as caring friend or loved one is to enter this painful process and be fully present to the bereaved when you are together. You cannot guide them through it; instead, be guided in your response by what they are going through.

*Many who mourn the death of a child require special help.* Bereavement counselors are mental health professionals who specialize in therapy for those struggling with their grief. Organized groups of bereaved parents also gather to support each other; Compassionate Friends is a national organization with over six hundred parent groups throughout the United States. Some congregations have organized their own groups to help with grief. Other parents in the community who have suffered the loss of a child will likely respond individually and usually provide tremendous support.

Resources are available to assist the family facing such tragic loss. (See the Appendix.)

I began this chapter with the story of seven-year-old Tommy, whose vibrant life was cut short by cystic fibrosis. I am happy to report that Tommy's parents survived his illness and death with their beautiful, creative personalities and marriage intact. As expected, their pain lasted years and, with many of us, they still mourn Tommy's loss. But they made it. They now have another delightful son, and I treasure their strength, happiness, and friendship.

The human spirit is amazingly strong and resilient. With faith and friendship we can survive almost anything. You are an agent of survival when you reach out to those who grieve. Not only can you supply friendship, the love you share will bolster their faith.

# 9

# With the Terminally Ill

Early in the morning this Thanksgiving day, I awoke to the sounds of the excited children and industrious adults of my family. I closed my eyes and thanked God for his blessings.

One blessing involved a young family to whom we are particularly close. Their daughter was born with a rare disease, a tumor growing inside her spinal cord. After she was diagnosed several years later, she underwent a delicate and risky operation. But hopeless surgeons closed her incision back up once they saw how severe the tumor had become. All the doctors could promise was to keep her comfortable for whatever time she had left. So an incurable disease became a death sentence to a little one when others her age were beginning kindergarten.

But her parents and two networks of practitioners, one of prayer and the other of medicine, had not yet surrendered her to the perverse cells choking out her life. Another medical expert emerged thousands of miles away. With the spiritual and material support of caring friends, her parents literally carried their daughter to him. The doctor agreed to attempt another major operation, apparently her last chance and hope. It was successful! Truly they had much to be thankful for on this happy Thanksgiving.

If you have a friend or family member facing a terminal illness, I urge you to adopt a perspective of hope. Avoid phony bravado, which is simply a way for people to distance themselves from the suffering they encounter in the critically ill. I have found a spirit of hope even among those for whom recovery is out of the question. Often I have left a bedside questioning whether I could possibly have done as much for that dear person as he or she did for me. Their hope shines through pain and tears and is a brilliant testimony to faith and love.

## Terminal Illnesses

Many of us have older relatives or close friends suffering with Alzheimer's disease, which ravages the mind with a cruel senility, then advances to the body. While we have seen remarkable progress in medical treatment and cures of the many forms of cancer, Alzheimer's disease continues to attack older people, largely unabated.

Another killer is on the march. The "human immunodeficiency virus" (HIV) that causes AIDS (acquired immunodeficiency syndrome) destroys the cells that protect us from disease and can hide like a time bomb in cells it doesn't destroy. A decade ago the first victim of AIDS known to me in our community was a preschool child. Experts fear that the majority of future cases of AIDS will be among young people. The deadly results of their indiscriminate sexual activity will not be known for years, for symptoms appear on an average of eight years after infection.

Life-threatening diseases (and there are many, many others) can attack any person of any age, including those close to us. Although we can acknowledge that possibility intellectually, emotionally such thoughts are unacceptable. We are understandably terrified, and some tremble even to say the word *cancer*. Too often, we readily slip into a mode of self-protection at the cruel expense of someone close to us who is struggling with a killer disease.

When dealing with a terminal illness, you need special grace and courage. Along with your listening skills, you should know some specific information and practical tips to help you show that you care.

*Some terms you may hear.* A medical dictionary helps from time to time as you practice caring friendship. The patient and his family may begin to use medical words to describe illness, conditions, and treatment. Here are a few terms you may hear during your visits.

A *terminal illness* is a condition that likely will result in death. A *chronic illness* is a condition that will likely never go away, may gradually increase its wearing down of a patient, and could in the long term be a cause of death.

A *malignancy* or a *malignant tumor* is a cancerous growth that must be removed or stopped in its tracks to remove its threat to life. *Metastasis* or *metastasized cancer* is cancer that has spread from its origin to other parts of the body. A tumor tested and determined to be noncancerous is called *benign*. The testing of tumor tissue to make a diagnosis is called a *biopsy*.

Regular *blood tests* are done on many cancer patients to check for the presence of cancer cells, often to determine the effectiveness of treatment. The *bone marrow* of patients with leukemia and some other cancers is similarly tested. A dear friend regularly telephones me after each periodic blood test so we can celebrate the good news of her continuing cure.

Cancers are usually treated in one of four ways, or a combination of any of the four: *surgery* to remove tumors and surrounding damaged, diseased tissue; *radiation therapy*, x-rays concentrated on tumors to remove them by burning; *chemotherapy*, using powerful chemicals and drugs that, when set loose in the bloodstream, attack cancer cells; and *hormone therapy*, a recent treatment in which human hormones are injected into the bloodstream, a treatment similar to chemotherapy. Powerful *drug therapy*, much of it in the experimental stage, is used to treat AIDS.

The happiest term of all is *remission* , which literally means that all disease cells have been "remitted," purged. Some remissions are permanent, and the physicians declare the patient cured after the passage of time. Some remissions are temporary but can be induced again with treatment.

Some treatments produce *side effects*, which are

usually temporary. A number of my friends in radiation therapy complain of nausea. Some undergoing chemotherapy lose their hair, at least temporarily. Drugs are often prescribed to assist with some side effects as well as to manage the severe pain associated with many of these diseases.

If in the course of discussion your friend or loved one uses a term you don't understand, don't be afraid to ask for a definition. Your friend wants you to understand her condition and won't be offended by your questions.

*Does the patient know the severity of the disease?* Most likely, yes, if he wants such knowledge. Most doctors now acknowledge the patient's "right to know" (and the related rights to get things in order, to make peace with others, and to say good-byes). Of course, the patient may also ask not to be told. Even with full medical explanations, the patient may or may not understand or accept the knowledge. And certainly it is his or her right to choose whether or not to tell you or discuss it with you. Many terminally ill persons try to "protect" those they love from the truth; I've known even young children in their final hours of life who try to keep their parents' spirits up by fabricating a better version of what's going on.

As little as twenty years ago, the medical community usually did not inform terminally ill patients of their condition. As a result, trust was destroyed between the patient, his loved ones, and the doctor at a time when trust was needed most. Usually such lies and game-playing protected not the patient but the medical professionals and relatives, who did not want to deal with the patient's hurt and grief. The studies of Dr. Elisabeth Kubler-Ross, however, revolutionized our attitudes toward the terminally ill.

*Where does the patient spend her final days?* As a result of Dr. Kubler-Ross's studies, not only were the terminally ill treated with more dignity and honesty, but they were also included in the decision-making process regarding options of treatment. The patient can now choose whether or not to receive treatment and can choose where that treatment is given. Whenever possible, the medical community honors the patient's desires.

Most people who suffer lengthy, debilitating illness yearn to leave the institutional setting of the hospital for the familiarity and comfort of home. The hospice movement evolved in response to that desire. First used in England, hospices are homes for the terminally ill. Stripped of most of the regimentation and regulation of a hospital, hospices have open visiting hours and allow children and sometimes even pets to visit. The large rooms comfortably hold family and friends for lengthy visits, and loved ones are allowed to stay at the bedside of the patient in the final hours of her life. Finally, hospice nurses are usually sympathetic to the relaxed "homey" atmosphere of the hospice and are trained to be caring listeners.

The hospice movement also has enabled patients to stay at home for their final days by providing nurses and other care givers who regularly visit to assist patient and family with medical treatment and emotional issues. As a result, terminally ill persons may now die in the comfort of their own homes, surrounded by those who love them most. It is the last gift a family can give a dying loved one on this earth.

Some hospital oncology (cancer) wards function like a hospice. Some convalescent hospitals likewise have special units for terminally ill patients. Whether in home, hospice, hospital, or convalescent hospital, a close friend or loved one will treasure your presence and appreciate your willingness to share the measure of time remaining to him.

### Dr. Elisabeth Kubler-Ross and the "Five Stages"

No individual has contributed more to our understanding of the terminally ill person than Dr. Elisabeth Kubler-Ross, the Chicago psychiatrist. Her now classic book, *On Death and Dying*, has helped countless doctors, nurses, clergy, families, and friends better care for, listen to, and understand the terminally ill. I will summarize her teaching, but you may want to read her entire book for more information.[1]

Just two decades ago, Dr. Kubler-Ross and her work with dying persons was met with great hostility, particularly from many of her fellow physicians and psychiatrists. The medical community is committed to fight death at all costs, and they viewed with suspicion Dr. Kubler-Ross's focus on the process of death. Finally, however, her studies of the terminally ill revolutionized the way patients were treated. Patients were given information and control over their treatment, and doctors and nurses began to treat them with respect and to allow them to die with dignity.

One of Dr. Kubler-Ross's important breakthroughs

was her theory of the stages of grief. After interviewing two hundred terminally ill patients over a three-year period, she identified five emotional stages of the dying person: denial, anger, bargaining, depression, and acceptance. Not all dying patients exhibit all five stages; neither do they all follow the same order. Let's look at the five stages in more detail.

*Denial.* It is natural for us to reject bad news. In my own counseling with persons who have just learned that they have a terminal illness, I've usually encountered denial: "The doctors must be wrong. I feel okay. In fact, I just jogged four miles today."

While for most patients denial is a short-term phase, a few patients of Dr. Kubler-Ross denied their real condition to the last. More common is for a dying person to fluctuate between moments of firm denial and growing awareness of reality. People who are terminally ill may also choose to deny the negative diagnosis to some persons and speak in more realistic terms with others.

Always listen fully to what a terminally ill person says as he comes to terms with his approaching death. Do not extract such conversation, however. As with all effective listening, take your cues from the one you seek to support, following his lead in setting the agenda.

*Anger.* "Why me?" is the logical next question once a man or woman stops denying the diagnosis of a terminal illness. Dr. Kubler-Ross describes feelings of anger, rage, envy, and resentment. I once worked for a professional colleague who was an impossible boss. Increasingly, he became less patient, and no matter how hard or long I worked, he always demanded more. One of his most-used statements was "Hurry. We don't have time to waste. People are dying!" His irrational pushing and cajoling made sense a year later, when he died of leukemia.

Anger may be directed at doctors, family, friends, and coworkers. Skilled and sensitive doctors, nurses, and chaplains recognize such outbursts as a necessary, normal release of emotional pressure; others deal with such anger by labelling the patient a "management problem" and treating the patient with contempt and neglect. Anger is a normal, appropriate release of pained feelings that friends and loved ones can expect in their conversations with a terminally ill person. Listening attentively and being present through the anger stage may require heroic patience and courage. But those who are dying deserve some heroes.

*Bargaining.* A bedridden young woman suffering from a cancer said to me, "If God will heal me, I'll work hard and give everything I can to the poor." A middle-aged man with advanced lung cancer told me, "If I get better, I'll stop smoking and take better care of my health." Dr. Kubler-Ross speaks of "bargains" that help a patient in the short term—"If I can just make it until my grandson's wedding, I'll be happy." I've seen very weak persons at death's door hold on for a special visit from a loved one or for some significant family event, then die soon after. As a stage, bargaining may last only fleeting moments in the emotional progress of a dying person and may often be private between the patient and God.

*Depression.* The terminally ill suffer declining health and strength, deteriorating physical appearance, increasing bills and financial pressures, loss of employment and subsequent loss of income, neglect by friends and colleagues, and impending separation from those they love most. Any one of these trials could cause a person to fall into a depression, and the terminally ill usually need to struggle with all of them. Once denial no longer protects the mind, anger no longer finds the energy to fuel it, and bargaining fails to draw a response, depression begins.

Many do not make it beyond this fourth stage of depression. Others use it to take care of inner issues without outside interference. Later they once again reach out to the world and move to the fifth stage, acceptance. But friends of the terminally ill should be prepared to ride out the depression, maintaining continuous contact. In my own work I have seen terminally ill patients come out of their depression and, with thankfulness, enjoy the time they have left with their loved ones.

*Acceptance.* Moving into the stage of acceptance takes a great deal of time. During this stage, the seriously ill person quietly makes peace in his or her heart with God, people, and personal affairs.

A friend and mentor of mine died earlier this year after a long bout with leukemia. In her final days on this earth, she was too weak for visits except by her closest family and trusted clergy. In a weak voice she told me that she was ready to die, unafraid of death, and grateful for her life and loves. She relaxed. She slept. She gradually, quietly, peacefully slipped away, her family at her side.

## Caring Approaches to the Terminally Ill

The unique humanity of a friend or loved one with a deadly illness is at risk as much as her physical health. I recall workers in the large New York City hospital where I trained referring to "the leukemia in bed 12." I'm sure these doctors and nurses were trying to protect themselves from their own fear of death. Nonetheless, I'm happy to say that over the years the responses of professional care givers to the terminally ill have improved with better training and understanding of their plight.

Many of us withdraw from the dying, even from close friends and relatives. Why do we hold back? Do we have an irrational fear of "catching" the disease? Do we feel emotionally unable to face death? Do we fear the emotions of a dear one who is dying? A terminally ill person faces not only physical deterioration and the end of life but even the loss of significant, supportive relationships.

You have the special opportunity to improve the precious last days of someone you care about by affirming him or her as a person who is valued and loved. Such relationships are at least as important to a dying person as any medical treatment.

*Be regular and constant in your caring for the long term.* Commit yourself to this significant relationship, as long as you are wanted and needed, to the end. To keep yourself from "slipping away," make a schedule for which days you'll write, telephone, or visit. You may want to create a calendar with other family and friends of the patient so that the "station" at his or her bedside is regularly filled by someone who cares. Encourage others to see the ill person through, either to death or, hopefully, to full recovery.

*In-person visits are most helpful.* While other kinds of communication are important, nothing prevents isolation from others and compensates for separation from activities better than your "being there." Some of my more mature and more honest friends who live alone tell me: "I need a hug." Touch is important. Hug your friend. Hold or shake his hand. Nothing is more important than physically being there for your friend.

*Look for little practical things you can do.* Sometimes doing even the smallest, easiest chore makes an entire day better for a seriously ill friend. You may read a favorite Bible passage out loud, share news from your circle of friends, offer to dust and straighten up the sick room, comb your friend's hair, or any number of other small things. Nothing delighted my dear grandmother more than when I would read letters from relatives all over the country and then write them replies as she would dictate.

Whenever possible, offer to take your loved one out to lunch, to a gathering of old friends, or to a church service. A day out can be the most tremendous spirit-builder of all.

*As always, be a good listener.* The very best therapy you can give someone facing death is to allow him or her to talk about it. Don't cut off the conversation when it gets difficult. Instead, keep on listening and drawing out feelings if the suffering person seems eager to share with you. You may well be the only person she trusts enough to open up to or the only person caring and courageous enough to sit and listen. However, don't be hurt if your friend does not share her feelings with you. Your offer and sincere willingness to listen may be gift enough. Be sensitive to your friend, and be guided by the cues she gives.

Your every caring contact with a terminally ill friend or loved one bestows a gift of love beyond anything you could know. And your own precious life becomes more meaningful in the process.

# — 10 —

# At the Hospital

I am writing this in my hospital room during the first overnight hospitalization of my life (not counting the days following my birth). For the last two days, I have been passing a kidney stone, a most painful process.

A sharp little pebble of uric acid is traveling from my kidney, through the urinary tract. For the first several hours my doctors could not give me any medication that might mask the symptoms and hinder their diagnosis. I remember the ordeal of riding to the hospital in the car and checking into the emergency room on a busy weekend night. At that time all I wanted was to stop the pain, and if not that, to be alone and quiet in a darkened room.

Obviously, I did not welcome hospital visits during my twenty-four hours of sharp pain. Only someone who loved me as much as my wife does could have withstood my unkind responses to her every well-intentioned attempt to help. I'm sure my sentiment would be shared by a woman in the advanced stages of labor as well as by anyone the day after a major surgical operation (often the most difficult day). I remember calling on one church member in the hospital whose back was so sensitive following surgery that even my knee slightly brushing against the outer bed frame caused painful discomfort.

So, how do you approach a friend in the hospital? When do you visit? What should you do once you are there? We turn next to these practical matters.

### Before You Go to the Hospital

*Begin on the telephone.* Assuming you are a close friend or relative, plan a visit. Telephone first. Perhaps you were notified of your friend's hospitalization by his spouse or other close relative; ask that person if visits are welcomed, perhaps even needed, at the present. If not now, when? You also often get good guidance from the patient's nurse; call the hospital and ask for the nurse caring for your friend. When you are certain the patient is up to receiving telephone calls, you may even telephone your friend directly. That call itself expresses your loving concern as well as helps you decide if you should appear in person. If you are going to visit, ask your friend if he needs anything brought from home.

When you are ready to visit, phone the hospital before leaving home to confirm visiting hours. Be sure your friend is allowed visitors; not only are there individual patient room restrictions, but special units like intensive care or coronary care strictly limit who may visit and when. In large medical centers, it also helps to know where you are headed, how to get there, and even where you can park. Calling ahead may save you embarrassment as well as wasted time and energy if your friend has been transferred or discharged or if his condition has changed and along with it, rules for visiting him.

**Understand the institutional setting of a hospital.** Although there are individual differences and philosophies, hospitals are institutions with rules and regulations. The chaplain of a large hospital used to joke that the nurse who ran the maternity ward acted like a Marine sergeant-major. Out of necessity, hospitals are fortresses of policies and procedures, with personnel to enforce them.

A good hospital, of course, develops its management practice around patients and helping them get well. There is a reason, for instance, that the nurse removes the bouquet you brought your neighbor—she's recovering from an asthma attack!

Of the various professionals ministering to a patient, nurses are the most significant care givers. Physicians and surgeons may come and go, but the patient's assigned nurse must remain available and responsive. The nurse can be your best guide and resource as you care for a loved one. If a nurse keeps information close to the vest, there is probably a reason. If a nurse advises you to respond in a certain way to the patient, consider her counsel carefully. Especially in lengthy hospital stays due to chronic or terminal illness, nurses get to know the patient and those who love him and become special resources to both.

Unfortunately, due to budgetary restrictions in most hospitals and a shortage of nurses, the number of nurses has declined, and fewer are available to sit and chat with patients. Continuity of care may also be disrupted; a different nurse may be assigned every day. This means your regular visits to hospitalized friends and relatives are more important than ever.

***Work on your own feelings about hospitals and hospitalization.*** Fear, again, is our biggest obstacle to caring for our hospitalized friend. Many of us are terrified of hospitals—rarely for any rational cause. We know that most people sail through hospitalization and return to active lives. We know that hospitals often provide the setting for the miraculous—birthing or saving a life. Certainly, no sane person wants to suffer a condition that leads to surgery or other medical procedures; no one wants to have his body tinkered with or invaded; no one wants to be sick. Perhaps fears come from such thoughts. But don't let your fears stop you from standing by your loved one. As in any crisis, the emotional signal that tells you, "Run!" also says, "Stay."

Many of our fears come from the unknown. Often, we can lessen our fears by naming them. For example, you may fear the bewildering maze of machines, tubes, and monitors hooked up to your friend. When you visit, find out the purpose of each piece of equipment, and you will feel more comfortable with their presence.

In chapter 1, I described my internship as a chaplain in a large hospital. One of the major goals of my internship was to get over my fear of hospitals. It worked. I no longer get a queasy pain in my stomach when I visit a hospital. Obviously, for pastors and others who must spend a lot of time in hospitals, working through such fears is a professional necessity. In my case it took a lot of work and time. My first assignment included the dermatology ward where rare skin diseases were treated; the head nurse laughed at how often I washed my hands, but said every doctor and nurse did the same in the beginning.

The way to get over your fears of the hospital or any other place that makes you anxious is to get in there and do what you have to do. Certainly, as you focus on the need of a friend or relative, your love for that person helps you rise above much of your anxiety.

I've encountered some lame excuses through the years for not visiting someone in the hospital, even when it may be a final opportunity to be with a loved one in this life. I've also seen a lot of remorse. Visit for the sake of your relationship with someone special to you. Hopefully, if you've read this far, even if you've hung on to such excuses, you're ready to discard them for the sake of the people you care about.

*Time your visits.* Earlier I mentioned telephoning to determine whether you should visit in the hospital and when. Check on visiting hours and any special schedule or requirements if your dear one is in a special unit of the hospital.

Determine how long you will visit. If the patient is in an acute phase, in a lot of pain, or in critical condition, your visit should be very short—unless your friend asks you to sit out part of the struggle with him.

The day after surgery, the hours before childbirth, and the process of passing a kidney stone are examples of an "acute" phase accompanied by much discomfort. If the patient wants anyone with him, he or she will decide who it will be.

If your friend will be in the hospital for a long time, she may welcome longer visits, but let her initiate them. Some people truly prefer to be alone most of this time. Coordinate your visits with other friends and family members so that the patient doesn't get too many visits one day and none the next. Sometimes families like to keep a vigil at the bedside of a member and set a schedule so someone is always there.

**Bring a gift.** Leaving a gift behind helps you to "extend" your visit, reminding your friend that you were there. You could bring a card, book, or flowers. Small floral arrangements are usually best, since hospital rooms are small. Before you buy flowers, however, check to see that the room has no restrictions on them—as in hospital wards for patients with respiratory ailments. Gifts of personal items are often appropriate. Gifts of food or drinks may be inappropriate if the patient is on a special diet. If the patient is about to go home, you may want to deliver the gift there so it won't have to be transported by the patient and his family.

Leaving a token of love helps the patient recall your visit in the following days. You needn't buy anything expensive; in fact, most hospitals warn against leaving any valuables in the room. Often I've taken a flower from our garden in a modest vase or a picture drawn by one of my children. These served the purpose of making the patient's room a little cheerier and reminding someone special to us that we care.

**You may need to know the routines surrounding surgery.** If you are a close family member, it will help you to know the schedule and procedures relating to an operation. The day or days preceding surgery are filled with tests, consultations with doctors, and various preparations. The night before surgery, there may be medications to take, and usually there is nothing by mouth ("N.P.O." may appear on signs on the door and headboard) after a certain hour, often midnight. The doctor may order a sleeping tablet to relax the patient and ensure a good night's sleep. Increasingly, hospitals administer all of the above on an "outpatient basis," the patient not checking into the hospital until very early on the day of surgery. The "outpatient" may need to check in before dawn the day of the operation. You can become a real hero by offering to drive!

About an hour before the operation, a nurse usually administers an injection to relax the patient and dry the mouth and digestive system. The patient will not have had so much as a drink of water since the night before. People respond differently to this injection, but most become groggy. As a pastor I often try to visit one hour before surgery is scheduled for a prayer. Any meaningful conversation must take place before this injection. After the injection, the patient needs to lie back, close her eyes, and relax. While it may be helpful to the patient to have a loved one close at hand during that final hour before surgery, it must be someone who can sit quietly and not need to be entertained. I have often taken a briefcase full of work with me into this setting. I sit and work close to the patient; we are together without my disturbing her rest.

For the sake of modesty, the nurse may ask you to leave the room at certain times, such as during the injection and when the patient is being moved from the bed into a gurney (a raised stretcher on wheels) for transportation to the operating room.

You may be allowed to walk alongside the gurney to an elevator or the door of the surgery area. When you say your farewells, encourage your loved one with a confident smile.

Patients in most large hospitals are taken into a holding room, then to a preparation room just outside the operating room to begin anesthesia. Close family members are directed to an area to wait out the operation and to receive word from the doctor when the operation is over. Those waiting then find out the status of the patient and when and where they can see her.

Surgical patients usually spend some hours in a recovery room where they are closely monitored while they fully awaken from anesthesia. It is standard procedure in some kinds of surgery for the patient to be taken from the operating room to an intensive care unit. Also, if it is late on a Friday or anytime on a Saturday or Sunday, the recovery room is probably not staffed; surgical patients then are routinely placed for a time in intensive care.

If you see the patient at all in the hours right after surgery, it will be only briefly, enough time for some mutual reassurance, a smile or a tear. Most likely, the groggy patient will not remember that visit in the future; in fact, some patients recovering from some kinds of operations do not recall many early visits. Remember, the day after surgery is often the most uncomfortable; time your visit (or stay away) accordingly.

## Practical Suggestions for Hospital-Room Visiting

You've called ahead, timed your visits, perhaps brought something for the patient. Now you are on his floor approaching his room.

*Knock before entering.* If the door is closed or you find the patient asleep, check with a nurse. You may find a nurse on private duty, caring only for your patient; more likely you'll find the nurse assigned to him at the nearest nurse's station. If the patient cannot be disturbed, you may want to leave any card or gift you brought along with a note assuring him of your love and prayers. Or the nurse may advise you to wait a few minutes before the patient can see you.

*Enter cautiously.* Once in the room with the patient awake and receiving you, approach tentatively. Don't take a seat unless the patient invites you and only then if you think he means it. If a chair isn't offered, keep the visit very brief. Always stand or sit so that it's comfortable for the patient to address you; position yourself according to where he is facing. If there are two or more of you, try to stand or sit on the same side; some medications actually prevent the patient from turning from side to side in conversation without dizziness, even nausea. Rarely, if ever, is it appropriate to sit on the bed or to use the patient's bathroom.

*Take your cues from the patient.* The closer to that "acute" phase, the less likely the patient is up to extended conversation, even if he seems fine to you. He also may be heavily drugged, which also decreases the patient's ability to focus and concentrate.

Watch carefully for signs of how long to stay and how complicated to get in dialogue. Don't bombard the patient with questions; to him it will feel more like a cross-examination than loving concern. Look for signs, both verbal and nonverbal, of the patient's comfort or discomfort.

*Don't allow the patient to become your "host."* Your visit has gone downhill if suddenly your friend assumes the role of host, making you comfortable, being animated for you, entertaining you. The patient is in the hospital because medically she needs help. Some people have a hard time being dependent and may try to put up a facade of being able to take care of themselves. Also, a patient is more likely to play host to less familiar visitors.

Graciously exit if your visit is causing the patient to become your host. Such visits can be hurtful, especially to a person recovering from major surgery or receiving heavy medication. The patient may pay the toll for such a visit the next day.

*Some diagnoses and treatments cause severe emotional pain.* In certain medical cases, the patient experiences grief. Any diagnosis that significantly changes your dear one's lifestyle (such as a chronic disease forcing retirement or transfer to a nursing home) or life expectancy (an untreatable cancer) or self-image (a mastectomy or amputation) will trigger a natural and appropriate grief response. If you visit at such a time, you will very likely encounter denial or anger. Sharpen your listening skills and draw on your courage and perseverance as you bear the bad news with your suffering friend.

## Following Up

*Discharge from the hospital can produce anxiety.* I found it somewhat unnerving to be discharged from the hospital following my recent kidney stone episode. At the hospital I had expert doctors and nurses who relieved my pain and took care of me. But what now? What if the pain starts again? How will I ever take care of the work that has been piling up since I've been sick? How large will my medical bills be?

In addition to anxiety about leaving the security of the hospital for the real world, the move home from the hospital is physically tiring. Be aware of how exhausted the former hospital patient will be on the day of returning home. It's not a good day to visit, but there may be something you can do to help if you are available.

*Don't forget the person recuperating at home.* If your friend or relative will be laid up at home for some time, don't forget to visit there. Away from the hospital and on the road to recovery, he may be lonely and impatient, ready for a visit and some extended conversation. People often receive considerable attention in the hospital and none at home. If housebound, even more if bedridden, your friend may be going stir crazy.

He may enjoy playing a game or doing a project together. Write and call frequently, too, and encourage other friends to do the same.

*Remember the patient's family.* They are suffering, too. Reach out to them. Perhaps you are in a position to be of special help, like baby-sitting so the patient's husband can visit her in the hospital. Often, there are tense periods when the patient's family must wait, perhaps during surgery or outside a coronary care unit. Your presence, if welcome, may be the greatest gift they could have at such a time.

Indeed, you may not even know the patient but be close to her spouse, parent, or child. The serious illness or surgery of one member ails an entire family. They may need your loving care as much as the patient. I know how difficult my recent hospitalization was on my wife and children—how it frightened my eight-year-old son to find me writhing in pain on the floor, how it taxed my wife to wait hours outside the emergency room for word of my condition, how it distressed my younger son to awaken to the news of my hospitalization the next morning. How grateful we are to our friends and neighbors and the teachers at our children's schools for their thoughtfulness, compassion, and prayers in seeing us through our days of crisis.

Loving friends are an important part of the hospital caring team. I'm certain they enhance the healing process for the patient and his immediate family.

# In Crises of Aging

In addition to the ravages of midlife, we post-World War II "baby boomers" share another thing in common: a growing concern for our aging parents. Increasingly, I find professional and personal time filled with conversation about how to do the right thing by our elders.

A late-evening telephone call from friends my age repeated a typical theme. Mother lives alone a hundred-plus miles away from the children who called me. Her home in a lovely retirement community is becoming more than she can manage, and she is making noises about moving into a church-related home for the aged. Although slowing down physically, she is mentally alert. A son who lives closer to her than the rest of her family doesn't want her to move, saying he wouldn't visit as much because of the distance. How far, my friends ask me, should they go in encouraging her move? And is the church home the best place for her?

Those of us who truly care about our parents and grandparents struggle as we deal with the emotionally-charged decisions and crises surrounding aging. We are, of course, blessed to have these generations with us. Improvements in health care guarantee better treatment of disease, slowing down of aging, and longer life spans. So, we must expect to face tough decisions for decades to come.

## Difficult Adjustments for Older Persons

Although the crises of the elderly are similar to those of everyone else, some of their particular problems cause them and us anguish. Among them are decreasing ability to manage one's own affairs and changing living arrangements.

*Managing personal affairs.* Age alone does not determine a person's capacity to manage the business of daily life. At eighty-three, my wife's grandfather could not attend her college graduation because he was on his honeymoon, managing quite well, thank you! Nevertheless, many older persons do suffer a lessened ability to manage personal business. When an aging person fails to recognize the need for help, those closest to him or her face a difficult problem. In addition to simple arrangements (such as joint bank accounts), creation of a "durable power of attorney" for health care, and living trusts, the law provides a way for us to protect people who cannot care for themselves—even against their wishes.

In California, for example, a "conservatorship" may be created literally to "conserve" the assets of the person with a declining business sense; a "guardianship" is ordered by the court for the man or woman unable to see to basic, daily requirements of health and safety, thereby virtually requiring "parenting" by a guardian. When no one is available from the person's own close family and friends to assume these court-appointed duties, the office of the public administrator takes over. I recently officiated at a burial service for a former parishioner who had no next of kin; all arrangements were made by the public administrator. The conservator, guardian, or public administrator regularly reports to the court on the conduct of responsibilities. There may be variations, state to state, on these provisions for persons of "diminished capacity."

Obviously, giving up control over one's own future, voluntarily or involuntarily, traumatizes an older person. It is not exaggeration to call such loss a "death" of sorts.

***Changing living arrangements.*** Perhaps it is my age or the nature of my work or the real estate market or the age of my friends, but I find more and more persons of retirement age happily making changes in the type and location of their housing. There are so many choices. Whole communities have been built around the needs and desires of older citizens. On the downside, many of the most popular (and affordable) retirement communities are out of state, often removing parents and grandparents hundreds of miles away from family and friends, making visiting and in-person assistance more difficult.

The planned move to a condominium on the golf

course in Palm Springs or Palm Beach differs dramatically from the necessary move into a senior housing facility or a nursing home. I am meeting many older persons who are opting for the long-term comfort and security of large, beautiful, well-staffed retirement institutions. Many of these places are lively, with opportunities for creative, educational, and social endeavors. Recently, two of my retired clergy colleagues, residents of our church home "for the aged," met delightful women, also residents of the home, got married, and moved out! (I teased my friend, the executive director of the large facility, about this dangerous trend in his lively institution.) Of course, all of us who know these newlyweds are delighted for their joyful new lives.

To adjust successfully to a move, the aging person should take part in the decision. One couple I knew had to decide where the husband should go when he was hospitalized with a terminal illness. After a few days, the hospital planned to release him to a nursing facility. His wife and doctor fully discussed the needed move with him. Upon fully understanding the needs and options, he encouraged his wife to make the necessary arrangements, thereby maintaining his dignity, allaying her guilt, and keeping their marriage of fifty years alive.

## What to Do

*Work things out as a team.* My friends in the example above worked things out together with the doctor, hospital social worker, and administrators of the nursing home he entered. I'm afraid that many decisions that change the life of an elderly person do not reflect such teamwork.

During my college days, a princely English gentleman lived in a rest home in my hometown. Because he was known for his gentleness, kindness, and politeness, it came as a shock to many of us when he went (literally) berserk upon learning of a small increase in his monthly room and board. (His well-off son, who lived in another city, paid the modest rent, and he always found it to be fair.) The now mentally disturbed father was carted off to the mental health wing of a nearby hospital, a locked facility where he was restrained hand and foot in his bed. It wasn't until days later, when the old gentleman became so physically weak that he was moved into the Intensive Care Unit, that he was given some basic physical tests. The testing revealed a life-threatening deficiency of a vitamin which, when administered, cleared up not only his physical symptoms but his mental illness as well. He returned to the rest home, where once again he was the perfect, dapper gentleman.

In the case of that elderly man, the lack of teamwork and coordination among his family, nutritionist, physicians, and psychiatrist almost cost his life. Whenever possible, the older person, too, should be recruited for the team that is making decisions about his life.

Most communities also provide resource people for the team; for instance, local governments, religious organizations, and hospitals often have social workers or gerontologists (experts on the aging) to assist elderly persons and their families with various needs. Most of us

have access to nearby Meals on Wheels or other meal
and visitation providers for the elderly. If you don't
know where to look for these kinds of assistance, begin
by asking your family doctor or clergyperson to point
you in the right direction. Your telephone directory
likely lists city and county government offices as well as
volunteer, nonprofit organizations concerned with the
needs of the aging.

*Visit as often as possible.* The greatest gift you can
provide a lonely person is your presence, yet many older
persons are neglected. A parishioner complained to me
that since his mother's stroke, many of her friends had
"left her at the side of the trail." Elderly persons who
live alone and who cannot get out and around as much
as they would like particularly cherish visitors and, in
many cases, love entertaining them. Those who have
moved from their own home into a retirement facility
especially need regular visits. A friend of mine used to
visit his mother in a nearby nursing home every day,
which delighted them both. When possible, take older
persons out, perhaps to go visiting themselves. Take
children to visit their grandparents and others of those
generations; it delights the older folks and helps the
children develop compassion and caring. Older children
who can drive can visit on their own.

One of the most touching accounts of human
relationships in the Bible is the story of Ruth and her
devotion to her aging mother-in-law. Both widowed,
the older woman urges Ruth to move away and get on
with her life. In a tearful speech, Ruth declares: "Where
you go I will go" (Ruth 1:16). Both women receive

great blessings and happy surprises (even romance) because of their mutual respect and love.

*Listen the best you can.* Effective listening (chapter 4) and understanding grief (chapter 5) are regular refrains in this book. The dramatic change in lifestyle of an older person, increasingly restricted from activities he previously enjoyed, is a true loss. Grief is the natural and appropriate response to that change. Advancing age may also trigger "anticipatory grief," as one anticipates change or even death. Or the older person may just want to talk about death, not as an emotional "downer" but as a matter of business and planning. Many aging parents would like to discuss such plans with their children, but the children are emotionally unable to listen to them.

I once designed a class for two neighboring churches on planning for one's own death and funeral. Surprisingly, many adults of a wide span of ages attended the class. Many were older persons whose own families would not allow discussion of such final plans. These elders were relieved to have a forum in which to consider their desires and options. These were not maudlin folks, preoccupied with death, as their children feared. Rather, they were full of life and wanted to get such heavy matters as estate planning and memorial services dealt with and out of the way so they could live freely without those heavy issues hanging over them.

Listening, like visiting, is a precious and often rare gift to the elderly person you care about.

*Honor and enable dignity.* Above all else, our older relatives and friends, to their dying breaths, deserve to keep their dignity. Over twenty years ago, the People's Republic of China was admitted to the United Nations. When it came time to find housing for their ambassador and other officials, the Chinese refused to purchase buildings from which older persons would be evicted—a common practice in New York real estate. "In our culture, we revere the elderly and their wisdom," a spokesman explained. In other words, in their culture the dignity of the elderly is more important than convenience.

In whatever we do as individuals or as a society for our senior relatives and friends, let us leave their dignity intact.

## —— 12 ——

# In Financial Crisis and Unemployment

*E*conomists and governments struggle to define what constitutes a recession or a depression. Yet such words are easy to define in personal terms. If I am falling behind in paying my bills because of less income, I am living through a recession. If I lose my job and must drastically reduce my family's lifestyle, I am in an economic depression. Recessions and depressions are more than trends in the macro-economics of the nation or words in newspaper headlines. They are personal tragedies, losses that lead to further losses for people, often our own friends and loved ones.

In recent years an increasing number of my friends and relatives have struggled with financial tragedy. Two Beverly Hills parishioners, CEO's of Fortune 500 companies, were forced out of their positions in "hostile takeovers" of their firms. Older friends, closer to retirement, were suspiciously "laid off," their future pensions threatened. A clergy friend lost his position as president of a large nonprofit corporation and was out of work for two years.

Church members well into retirement years have been forced to move out of the area because their once-sufficient fixed incomes were reduced in value by inflation. Several families I'm close to, with sophisticated and financially successful breadwinners, faced bankruptcy following divorce. Numerous relatives and friends are still struggling to catch up following business reversals in the 1980s.

## A Problem That Can Grow

When I was a child, I couldn't resist pulling on a loose or snagged thread at the top of a knitted sock. With a major pull I could unravel several feet of thread, destroying the sock.

The loss of a job or investment or other primary source of income for a household can cause unravelling of family life. To describe the seriousness of potential additional losses, I sketch out below some results of such a loss. Even if your friend or relative never has to face such complications, he or she may panic, thinking that the worst is yet to come. However, it would never be appropriate for you to increase the anxiety by suggesting how things could get worse! Such examples are listed here to help you prepare for the maze of what you might encounter as you respond to someone in financial or employment crisis.

*The blow to confidence and self-esteem.* Psychologists have observed that, for many men—and, I would suspect, for many women—self-identity is wrapped up in the job. When two men meet for the first time, almost invariably the first question they ask is, "What do you do?" Sadly, many hardworking folks never develop fulfilling interests and activities beyond work. Have you noticed how many men die soon after retirement? For people whose self-image is tied up in their job or their income, losing that job may be a severe blow.

If the unemployed person was fired or "pushed out," or if the loss resulted from business or investment decisions gone bad, such feelings as guilt, anger, or depression (grief responses, in other words) would not be unusual. (See chapter 5 on the emotional responses of grief.) A worsening financial situation may lower self-esteem even further. When we hurt this way, our relationships with others can't help but be affected. And the hard work of looking for a new job or getting business problems solved is made even harder by the emotional drain.

*Compounding financial troubles.* A prolonged financial crisis may mean inability to make mortgage payments on the family home, pay college tuition costs for children, or qualify for the credit to make such payments. Credit cards may be used excessively to keep a particular lifestyle or "image" in the community. Group health, life, and disability insurance provided by an employer or one's own business may be lost.

*Impact on family members.* A spouse and children become anxious as they become aware of the impact (or possible or imagined impact) of a financial crisis. Money and attitudes about its use often cause strain in marriages. For this reason, I always raise money issues with couples in premarital counseling. Many marriages disintegrate when differences about finances are not resolved. Obviously, a significant drop in family income can trigger major conflict, even in healthier relationships. If one spouse overextends credit to maintain a particular lifestyle (a situation I've observed in Beverly Hills), domestic troubles follow. I've known friends who have hidden their financial crises from their families and allowed everyone to continue a high level of spending until it was too late.

Children, too, are affected by a financial crisis. Most children (like most adults) hate change and worry about the changes that financial pressures bring. Teenagers may worry that they'll lose status if they can no longer afford certain clothes. Children may suffer emotionally and socially if more drastic measures are required, such as moving to another state or community.

### Possible Caring Responses

One of my friends was helping homeless persons when she discovered her own cousin, an elderly woman with whom she'd lost contact years before, living on the streets. My friend immediately took her relative in and began the challenging process of helping her. You may or may not be called upon to face the extreme poverty of someone so close to you. You may or may not be in a position to respond with your own resources. But let's begin with that possibility.

*Direct assistance.* In accordance with your circumstances and values, giving money or other direct assistance to friends or relatives in financial need is one possibility. My friend who discovered her relative on skid row was immediately certain of how to respond and for months remained committed to a tangle of problems. More likely, you and I will find easier ways to give direct help, such as preparing and delivering meals, baby-sitting while a relative searches for a new job, or providing transportation.

Obviously, for most of us, there are limits to how much we can do. Speak very clearly regarding those limits to yourself and to the person you are helping. ("I wish I could help with money, but since I can't, I would like to drive you to your new job for the next week.") Furthermore, think carefully before you offer certain kinds of aid, such as providing a job or lending money. If you provide a job, would it be temporary or permanent? What will you do if it doesn't work out?

If you choose giving money, I suggest you give it as a gift, without expecting a return. Whenever possible, avoid large loans or "investments." I have friends who loaned money, goods, and professional services for which they were never repaid. I've seen even worse results when financially desperate people have solicited "investments" for the miracle project that will solve all their problems. I have counseled pastorally with parishioners and clergy who have been injured personally by making such "investments." Approach all requests for loans and investments very cautiously, with wise and careful judgment.

*Keep in regular contact.* When a friend of mine, the CEO of a film company, lost his job, he was personally devastated by the lack of communication of significant friends, including me. His friends and I were scared off by his anxiety, hostility, anger, and frustration. When he sent me a newspaper clipping about how executives who have lost their positions are abandoned by friends, I apologized to him and resolved to keep in touch. I realized that he needed to express his anger and that I was one of the few he could count on for such listening.

Keeping in regular contact with a financially stressed friend means calling and visiting at least as much as when things were stable financially. If you had talked every day at work, you might check in daily by telephone. If you used to have lunch weekly, try to maintain that pattern—your treat if that doesn't harm your friend's dignity.

If your friend or relative resists your attempts to maintain your relationship, evaluate sensitively how much pushing you should do. If you are "put off" the first time you offer to get together, don't consider that a reason to duck out of the friendship for the duration of the crisis. (Be sure to express your sincere desire to meet in specific terms: "May I come by to see you tonight?") On the other hand, loyally persisting to maintain a friendship and inappropriately pushing your way into a situation where you may not be wanted or needed are two different things. Be especially sensitive to a colleague who needs to preserve dignity during a time in which his or her self-worth is under assault.

In addition to helping keep your friend's spirits up,

by keeping in touch you may be able to help your friend locate another job.

**Be alert to opportunities and resources.** In my professional life, at least, the best opportunities have resulted from caring friends and relatives sharing information with me and with prospective employers. Take my mother-in-law, for example.

In my last semester of seminary, my bishop back home in California notified me that there were not enough pastoral positions available to assign to everyone who was graduating. Since I thought we might have to stay out East, we mailed both sets of our parents a poor quality carbon copy of a letter of application that I'd sent to a church in South Carolina. The day my wife's parents received it, my mother-in-law was chatting with a pastor friend of my father-in-law before a dinner meeting. This friend mentioned that they were searching for an associate rector for his parish in a neighboring town. She told him about me and produced the smudged, error-ridden carbon copy of my letter. Eventually, I was offered that position, and we chose to go there. I never even received an acknowledgment of my original letter to the church in South Carolina!

Networking is crucial to finding a new job. Your friend should communicate with as many people as possible about his qualifications, experience, and the kind of work he'd like to find. He should also ask his friends to inquire on his behalf, thus building a larger network to help with the search. Not only might your participation in this network provide possible leads for employment, your regular communication will encour-

age your friend or relative to keep at the task of sending
out inquiries and resumes every day.

*Refer your friend to professional help when appro-
priate.* Various professionals and organizations serve
unemployed and financially troubled persons. If your
friend needs help finding a job, he should contact the
local unemployment office or register with an executive
search firm. If he needs help with organizing his
finances, he may use a nonprofit credit counseling
organization to help him budget and plan ways to pay
off his debt. If he is in dire financial need, many
churches and religious organizations may be able to
help, and he should also contact the state department of
unemployment and social services. Finally, if he needs
psychological or career counseling, he may receive help
from the company that displaced him (many offer "out-
placement" services for laid-off staff), from an executive
search firm, or from any other recommended counselor.

Friends and relatives struggling financially are not
alone. Walt Disney was forced to declare bankruptcy
more than once. My parents and grandparents and
millions of other folks worldwide suffered through the
Great Depression. That friend or relative struggling
with unemployment or financial loss is in good company
and, hopefully, will know your good company as well.

## — 13 —

# With Families Facing Breakup or Abuse

A caring friend like yourself may one day out of the blue hear a shocking revelation from someone you love:

- After thirty-five years of marriage, a close family friend announces: "I wanted you to know, Neal and I are getting a divorce."

- A colleague responds to your inquiry about his sister: "I don't know how she is. I haven't talked to my sister in ten months."

- A fellow volunteer in a youth program answers your inquiry about how his family is doing: "We are in bad shape. We just learned that all three of our children have been molested by their older cousin."

- A recently widowed friend who is worried that she is losing her relationship with her daughter says: "I just wrote her a letter telling her how disgusted I am with her choice of a fiancé."

How do we respond meaningfully to revelations like these? I am rarely speechless, as my wife will attest, but I find my mind and my mouth stalling in such encounters with those close to me.

One kind of crisis situation that will tempt you to back away, turn, and run is family problems. Your relationship will be emotion-charged with a loved one whose family is breaking up, who is alienated from one or more family members, or who is dealing with abuse. You may feel justifiably helpless. In some situations you may feel pulled into the middle of a battle in which you want to remain close to combatants on both sides. You will feel hurt, awkward, and frustrated. But if you expect and accept these feelings, you will be better able to deal with them, and you won't let them stand in the way of helping your friend.

## Finding Perspective in Domestic Warfare

Estrangement within families takes two major forms: the deterioration of the marriage relationship in separation or divorce, which breaks apart the family; and the alienation of one family member from another. Each of these is discussed in this section, followed by suggestions for caring responses. Abuse issues are discussed in a latter section of this chapter.

*Separation and Divorce.* In most states the law distinguishes between separation, legal separation, and divorce as progressive stages toward the total dissolution of a marriage. Often, sometimes with the advice of a counselor, a couple separates on a trial basis, to allow time for heated emotions to cool down before the couple tries to work things out. Or the trial separation may help them to test out living apart, seeing what divorce would be like. Legal separation is a further step leading to a final decree of divorce by the courts.

The process of breaking up a marriage is costly in many ways. Legal fees for court costs and lawyers are extremely expensive. Even in so-called no-fault divorce states, like my own state of California, where legal proceedings establishing blame are no longer required for divorce, property settlement and child custody battles can cost tens or even hundreds of thousands of dollars, depending on the financial and emotional stakes.

Police departments have on record horror stories of family disputes. Based on experience, most police departments consider a domestic dispute the most dangerous kind of call and routinely dispatch a backup officer to support the officer who deals with the disturbance. Occasionally, even law-abiding citizens can temporarily lose control when under extreme emotional pressure. I'll never forget the police entering the home of friends to remove a spouse during an especially bitter and potentially violent divorce proceeding.

Friends and relatives often feel they need backup as well. Usually each estranged spouse emotionally presents his or her side of the story with a mixture of compelling and questionable arguments. Often they attempt to get the friend or loved one to take a side, even to provide legal evidence for the court.

Of course, there are situations in which one spouse is more clearly the innocent victim. In cases of violence, destructive chemical abuse, and adultery, for instance, someone needs to take action.

No matter what has occasioned the divorce, your friend will likely react with shock, anger, and all the other emotions of grief. In a sense, she is responding to a death—the death of a marriage. Counselors and support group leaders tell us to expect such grief responses in any divorce. The circle of those mourning the death of this relationship will grow, from the spouse and children to all those who loved anyone in the family.

The children always suffer—and usually suffer most. Even in the best possible scenario, even if they suffer less in the divorce than they did in the most horrible, combative, dysfunctional family, they will suffer. Both teenagers and young children suffer equally. Often their grief centers on guilt: children of divorcing or divorced parents often blame themselves. Children also suffer the most in the legal system. They are too easily used as pawns, for child custody is a bartering chip in reaching financial settlements.

The startling and growing trend of couples divorcing after thirty or more years of marriage provides an unfortunate opportunity to observe the grief of grown children of divorcing parents. Maturity in years doesn't necessarily prepare a child to deal with the estrangement of parents. I've seen adult siblings take sides and become estranged from each other in such divorces. Young grandchildren obviously become bewildered as their extended family deteriorates.

One of my high school students told me, "Divorce is something that no book can describe. I have yet to find a book that showed or even remotely described my feeling of shock when I knew that I would never again be able to come home and say 'Hi Mommy, hi Daddy, how was your day?' Honestly, though, it was for the best because I could not bear to see them fight another moment. The only thing I've read about divorce that was on the nose was, unfortunately, that it is hardest on the children. The pain never goes away, but the fear of what might have been if they had stayed together compensates for it a little."

Those words reflect not only pain and loss but also reality and resolve. The resilient human spirit makes survivors of most of us. Given adequate time and support, adults and children pick up their lives and move on after divorce, even though many of them will never be the same again.

In some cases, happily, there is hope for reconciliation. Close friends and members of my church separated, dramatically and publicly, and divorce seemed certain. Issues they had worked on for years seemed irreconcilable even after their best attempts and professional counseling. The wife was no longer willing to live with such unresolved conflict over what she saw as vital and basic matters, so she left. She contacted an attorney immediately.

Friends closed in around both spouses to give support. Unfortunately, the support often hurt as much as it helped. For example, many friends chose to care for only one spouse or the other; few of us attempted to keep in touch with both. Also, instead of "holding up" the spouse, the friends often "tugged the spouse away"; friends, many of them divorced themselves, urged the couple to get divorced quickly. These responses helped "seal the fate" of that marriage. Or so it seemed.

But the husband resisted. He resisted the reality of his situation, the legal process begun by his wife, and the pressure of friends to "get on with the next chapter" of his life. He mourned and repented. Humbly (and humility had never before been his style) he repented to his wife repeatedly and asked for one last chance to improve their relationship through counseling. For whatever reason, she relented. After intensive therapy, they reunited and lived as they had vowed—until death parted them. Their example will live in many memories, for many years.

I've even had the joyous privilege of conducting marriage services for persons who had divorced years before and "found" one another anew. What a testimony to love's power to overcome estrangement!

*Alienation of Family Members.* In the powerful film, *Irreconcilable Differences*, the young daughter of highly successful, bickering parents sues them for divorce so as to be placed in the custody of her responsible, mothering, Hispanic nanny. I summarized the film as a sermon illustration one Sunday and a few days later was recounting the powerful story to a friend at lunch in a Beverly Hills restaurant.

By chance, the film's producers were seated at the next table! Overhearing our conversation, they told us about the audience's reaction to the film at its premiere. One of the producers noticed that many of her friends were getting up during the screening and heading for the lobby. Anxious about this strange reaction to her motion picture, the producer finally made her way to the women's lounge. There she found a number of women, representative of success in Hollywood terms, dabbing their eyes with tissues and lining up to use the pay phone to call home and check on their own children!

Unfortunately, the parents in the film do not respond as well to their neglected little daughter. In that sense, in many cases of alienation among family members, art imitates life.

Alienation does not discriminate according to age. Brothers and sisters rival one another at eight and at forty-eight. Parent-child estrangement is also ageless. Increasingly, adult children from dysfunctional families (like those who experienced an alcoholic parent or abuse) seek therapy at various stages of life, even after their parents have been dead for years.

Much of what we term the "runaway" problem in our country fails to acknowledge the "throwaways," teenagers who have been turned out of their homes and onto the streets by their parents. Because few of these adolescent runaways and throwaways can fend for themselves, becoming targets for various disasters, our society is increasingly sensitive to their needs and their alienation from their families.

Not all broken relationships in families are as dramatic as those described above, but many are at least as tragic and painful. For whatever reasons—historical, psychological, moral—some members of otherwise sound families maintain cool, cold, or no relationships with one or more relatives. Sometimes the original reasons for the break are barely remembered in the foggy past, yet the break continues unquestioned.

Of course, because we are imperfect human beings, most of our families have experienced conflict, which we have then addressed and healed. Happily, such healing can also occur where there have been years or even decades of estrangement. While we wait and pray for that kind of healing for friends and relatives struggling with alienation in their families, we can express our care for them in a number of ways.

## Caring Responses

*Accept any awkwardness or frustration.* You did not cause this problem, and you cannot solve it. If you are having a dinner party for all your relatives, including two estranged persons, do the best you can to provide a pleasant atmosphere, such as in arranging seating. But don't fault yourself if, despite your best intentions and efforts, a cold front and storm clouds develop near the warring parties. When confronted with the sad news of someone's relational breakup, don't fault yourself for your initial silence. You, too, will experience shock and grief in response to such sad news.

*Expect grief responses from your friend or loved one.* The death of a relationship or even its critical illness triggers grief, guilt, and anger, which may be directed your way. (See chapter 5.)

*Be a good listener.* Your active listening may be your greatest gift of caring. During the times I suffered through a broken relationship, nothing helped me more than sharing my feelings with someone I trusted. (See chapter 4.)

*Be supportive.* Personal support begins by being fully present to your loved one and by active listening that communicates: "I care, and I hear you." Support does not mean approving of your friend's thoughts or actions. Instead, it simply means affirming her as a person. Keep in touch as the grieving process continues; telephone or write between visits.

*Beware of encouragement that justifies your own life situation.* Unintentionally, unconsciously, you may have scars from relationships in your own life that cause you to give advice and comfort to others not to help them as much as to assuage your own feelings and justify your own decisions. For instance, when Joe considered leaving his wife, his divorced friends encouraged him. They exaggerated the benefits of divorce and minimized the problems, even though Joe's relationship and problems with his wife had no resemblance to any of their own.

*Attempt to maintain your friendships with each person in the conflict.* And realize that you may fail despite your good efforts. It may be very difficult to avoid being pegged on a particular side: "Any friend of his is no friend of mine." Yet when your friendship with those on both sides predates their conflict, try to maintain individual relationships with each. Even if you succeed, however, the "new" relationships will likely differ from each other and from the friendship you enjoyed with the couple (or family) before.

*Avoid "taking sides."* Avoid even the appearance of taking sides. You may feel closer to one estranged party, or perhaps you believe one of them to be right and the other wrong. But in the vast majority of cases, you risk complicating the problem by jumping into the fray. Pointing an injured or confused person to appropriate resources (such as professional counseling) is usually a better way to help him or her than jumping into the emotional cauldron yourself.

Friends and parishioners have put me in an awkward spot in child custody disputes by asking me to write a letter to the court recommending their personal qualities as a parent. When I have been close to both spouses and feel each is an effective and caring parent, I write the letter on behalf of the one requesting it and then offer to do the same for the other parent.

*Consider any legal and moral responsibilities.* Suppose your friend's fourteen-year-old son ran away from home after a major blow-up with his parents. The police have begun looking. The parents are becoming increasingly despondent. At sunrise, three days later, there is a knock at your front door. It is the runaway youngster, who asks to come in and begs you not to reveal his whereabouts. What should you do? Because of the legal and moral issues involved, I would try to convince the teenager to let his parents know that he is safe, and then work on getting them reunited.

Some situations with moral complications are less clear. For instance, you see your friend's wife out on the town with another man. What do you do with the information? Or what should you do if you suspect abuse? Think about the legal and ethical ramifications before you take any steps to help your loved one during a family crisis.

*Direct estranged friends and loved ones to appropriate help.* Most communities have professional counselors and support groups specializing in family relationships. The Appendix also lists helpful resources for addressing various family problems.

*Allow lots of time for healing to occur.* Resolving estranged relationships or grieving for those that cannot be resolved takes considerable time and work. Authentic caring requires patience and keeping in contact over the long term.

### A Word About Abuse and Domestic Violence

Abuse and domestic violence are major problems affecting millions of people. The statistics and estimates vary, but something like forty percent of us were abused as children, either physically, emotionally, or sexually. Because we tend to bury our heads in the sand, most of the cases of abuse are never confronted and exposed. The victims are left with terrible scars, and may themselves become abusers if left untreated.

Therapists and clergy are growing in awareness of the scope of child abuse, especially through counseling adult victims. Many abuse victims suppress their memories of childhood abuse and do not recall it until an event triggers the memories years later. Often other problems—in marriage or family, for instance—may be caused by childhood abuse. A clergy colleague of mine recently led a women's retreat where he needed to set aside the theme he had planned once the women started talking about their childhoods; almost every woman there reported being abused as a child.

We are also growing in our awareness of domestic violence, where one spouse physically assaults another. Most communities have shelters and "safe houses" as a refuge for those who have been attacked.

In my own work in child abuse, I am finding more and more people wanting to talk about it. There are adults who want to deal with issues from their own childhood, and there are parents who are concerned about the abuse of their own children or other children known to them.

Often child abuse causes estrangement between parents or between parent and child. Dealing with child abuse, even when the perpetrator is outside the family, can stretch a marriage's emotional capacity to the breaking point. And child abuse known to the parents and not attended to estranges the child from the parents, in the future if not immediately; I have counseled with a number of adults trying to deal with hostility toward parents who shrank from facing the abuse their children suffered twenty or thirty years ago.

This is frightening information, but it's real. Abuse is an issue in' your community, regardless of ethnic, racial, or socioeconomic makeup. How can you as a friend or relative respond when your instincts tell you to run and hide from such a horrible revelation?

Generally, you may follow the guidelines for responding to estrangement in families, with these four additions.

**Learn about abuse.** As a caring person, you need to learn enough about abuse and domestic violence to believe how prevalent and devastating these problems are. Accept what is reported to you as truth.

**Take claims of abuse seriously.** If you have a caring and trusting relationship with a friend, she may turn to you to confide her abuse. Children, too, may seek you out. At times they may reveal the abuse in a symbolic way, then back away from what they've said. Listen carefully to what they say and believe them. A critical moment for getting better is when the abused person recalls what happened to him or her and reaches out to share it with someone else. If you are that someone, your attentiveness and caring response helps your loved one—child or adult—continue to talk about his or her abuse and seek the help needed to get well. Such a moment calls for you to set everything else aside, listen, believe, and care. (See chapter 4.)

**Realize that you are in "over your head."** As a caring friend, you do not have the experience or the training to deal with abuse issues. You need to seek community and professional help for your friend or loved one. If you continue to act as a support for the victim, seek assistance for yourself as well, educating yourself on appropriate ways to respond to promote healing and well-being. (See chapter 15.)

**Consider the moral and legal implications.** In certain states specified professionals (like teachers, doctors, and counselors) are required by law to report cases of suspected abuse or neglect to child welfare authorities. Severe criminal penalties back up such laws; "mandatory reporters" face felony prosecution for failing to report in California. If you get your friend or relative to the right professional, reporting will follow. Also, you may need to get advice yourself as to whether or not you should report the abuse. In some cases, lives may be at stake. Your own conscience and instinct will assist you with such legal and moral questions.

Remember, you did not create these crises. You cannot solve them. But there are many people out there to help and support you and your hurting loved one.

# When Dealing
## with Chemical Dependency
## and Eating Disorders

When you are close to someone struggling with alcohol or drug abuse or an eating disorder, be prepared for some of life's most tragic and most miraculous experiences. Consider these two scenes.

The setting: early evening in the emergency room of a Los Angeles area hospital. I am standing with the anxious young children of a woman who is on the verge of death following an overdose of drugs mixed with alcohol. The children found their mother unconscious in her bedroom and called the ambulance. Thankfully, the paramedics arrived in time, and she is saved. But this woman has a history of abusing alcohol and prescription drugs, causing her children untold anguish, fear, and humiliation.

The setting: late afternoon in my church office in Beverly Hills. I am sitting with the same woman, now a highly regarded bank officer. Even her professional dress and air cannot disguise her nervousness. Glancing occasionally at some notes, she begins to apologize for specific times when she hurt me and my family. She speaks of that night, years ago, when I stood for hours with her children in the hospital emergency room while her stomach was pumped to save her from an overdose of drugs and alcohol. I am flushed with emotion, including embarrassment, as she asks my forgiveness and asks me to convey her apologies to my wife for the nights our family life was disrupted by her chemical abuse crises.

At first I was startled that she could recall so many times I had been drawn in to help her and her children. And I have been awestruck ever since by the miracle of her recovery. That afternoon, she had come to my office to work on Steps Eight and Nine of the "Twelve Steps" of Alcoholics Anonymous: "We made a list of all persons we had harmed and became willing to make amends to them all. We made direct amends to such people whenever possible."[1]

Let me repeat: When you are close to someone struggling with alcohol or drug abuse or an eating disorder, be prepared for some of life's most tragic and most miraculous experiences.

## Definitions

*Addiction.* Step One of Alcoholics Anonymous provides an excellent working definition of an addiction—to alcohol or any other substance or compulsion: "We admitted that we were powerless over alcohol—that our lives had become unmanageable."[2] This lack of control over a substance signals an addiction. Indeed, a friend is in trouble when a substance or compulsion takes control. He is like a car without brakes careening down a hill, destroying everything in its path before it smashes itself.

*Alcoholism.* Alcoholism is a disease, apparently genetic in its origin. An individual with alcoholism cannot consume any alcohol, just as a person with an extreme allergy to a particular food cannot consume that food without triggering illness. Alcoholism is more complicated than chronic drunkenness; an alcoholic has a physical as well as emotional dependency on alcohol. The disease is not the result of moral weakness, although it requires considerable moral strength to recover from it.

*Drug dependency.* A person is dependent on drugs when he loses control over his life to chemical substances. These substances may include tobacco, illegal drugs, prescription drugs, or household materials (like model airplane glue). While *addiction* means that the body has come to rely on a drug for physical well-being, *dependency* means that a person habitually uses a certain substance as an emotional crutch.

*Eating disorders.* These include out-of-control, compulsive overeating as well as anorexia and bulimia. An anorexic starves herself, while a bulimic "binges and purges," eating to excess and then vomiting to empty the stomach. Anorexia and bulimia create a complex of physical conditions that can be fatal, just as obesity can kill. Anorexia and bulimia almost always affect girls and young women, pertain to problems in self-image, and relate to issues involving significant males (father, boyfriend, husband). Often eating disorders may be linked to childhood abuse.

*Multiple abuse.* When an individual has a combination of the problems sketched above, he is involved in multiple abuse. For instance, many people abuse both alcohol and prescription drugs. Some drug addicts abuse different kinds of narcotics. Persons suffering with eating disorders might easily turn to alcohol or drugs to ease their pain. Many of my recovering alcoholic friends became chain smokers after they achieved sobriety. Perhaps you know smokers who quit, then put on a lot of weight as they ate compulsively to compensate for the lack of cigarettes.

Multiple abuse is common for those who have compulsive personalities, and treatment for it is similar to treatment for any one addiction. Usually, someone struggling with one or more addiction receives therapy, which deals with his underlying personality problems, or joins a Twelve-Step support group to help him stop his addictive behaviors.

### Treatment

Treatment for chemical dependency and eating disorders can range from stopping cold turkey to having lengthy and recurring hospitalizations. Most people can be helped with treatment that is somewhere in between such extremes. I will briefly sketch out some elements of current treatment.

*Bottoming out.* On the morning after a family party, an old friend of mine was confronted by his wife about his drinking. A heavy social drinker since college days, he was usually the life of the party. His drinking had caused him problems through the years, but he always believed he was in control of his drinking—until that morning. His wife told him how he had behaved the night before and how he'd made their children and her feel. He responded that he could not remember any inappropriate behavior. Gently, she told him that their young son had felt totally humiliated in front of their relatives and friends.

A grand jury indictment could not have stung him more. "She said I was humiliating the kids," he related to me later. "I haven't taken a drink since that day." He is now years into his sobriety and still the life of any party. But at the drop of a hat, he will share how his wife made him aware of what his drinking was doing to him and those he loved.

Alcoholics Anonymous (A.A.) calls this moment of awareness "bottoming out." It constitutes the First Step of A.A., the moment when an alcoholic recognizes that his or her drinking is unmanageable. Many alcoholics, including the founders of A.A., didn't hit bottom until they were nearly destroyed. A.A. meetings, therefore, try to create a "higher bottom" for attenders who are still drinking by inviting participants to share personal stories that show how far down life can go for an alcoholic who continues to drink.

Family members of persons dependent upon drugs or alcohol must often stand by and observe, even rejecting the natural instinct to rescue, as they wait for their loved one to hit bottom. The expression "tough love" is familiar to many parents of teenagers who abuse drugs and alcohol. Out of love and from many experiences of heartache, they come to a point where, having done all they can, they must let their child suffer the consequences of his or her problem, hopefully hit bottom, and then become ready to begin recovery.

One father I counseled had a son in his late teens who had a perennial problem with drugs and alcohol. His son had received numerous tickets and been in and out of court, counseling, and treatment programs. The father, a widower, vowed that he would never again bail out his son—either literally or figuratively. One Friday night just after midnight, the son called from the police station; he had been arrested for drunk driving and would be taken to the county jail. He begged his father to bail him out, saying that the inmates would beat him up and even threatening to commit suicide. But his father refused. Fortunately, his tough love won out. The son bottomed out in jail, and the court-ordered treatment programs that followed were successful.

Bottoming out was once seen as the necessary first step toward recovery. Somehow, the problem drinker has to come to the hard realization that his life is going down the drain if he continues to drink. Traditional A.A. wisdom declares that until an alcoholic bottoms out, little can be done. In recent years, however, a second approach has developed to get alcoholics (and people with many other kinds of destructive, compulsive problems) into programs of recovery—intervention.

*Intervention.* By definition, bottoming out usually doesn't occur until things get pretty bad. An alcoholic may do irreversible damage to his or her job, driving record, marriage, and liver before realizing that his drinking is out of control. Young adults with criminal records may ruin their chances to be accepted into college, to get a job, or to enter the military. Therefore, more and more people are deciding to intervene with the alcoholic before the situation becomes critical.

"Intervention" means that others, by virtue of their relationship or authority, intervene to get a chemically dependent or eating-disordered individual into treatment. By definition, this is an individual who hasn't yet come to grips with her or his destructive problems. Therefore, part of the treatment that follows the intervention is to force the person to become aware of her problem. Usually, interventions require that the person enroll in a residential treatment program.

Parents often intervene on behalf of their minor children. When Mom and Dad discover that their daughter is using cocaine, for example, they enter her in a treatment center with the help of a professional who specializes in adolescent intervention. Criminal court judges also have the authority to order an individual into a treatment program. Many families wait for such mandatory, legal intervention when their efforts to help their loved one have failed.

Sometimes friends conduct an intervention session, which is a sort of conspiracy of caring. In an intervention session, an alcoholic is confronted with his problem by family members, friends, business associates (especially his boss), a counselor, the family physician, a pastor, and anyone else whose relationship or authority would make his or her words compelling.

One of my friends once went through such a session. Ken was an executive for a large nonprofit organization. He was also a functioning alcoholic, meaning that his excessive problem drinking did not prevent him from getting his work done. But he was destroying himself in ways apparent only to his family and closest professional associates. Finally, some of these people stopped discussing the problem in hushed tones one-on-one and called a meeting of all the important people in Ken's life. Then they consulted a professional counselor who specialized in intervention. Together they set up a time when the intervention would take place.

On the day of the intervention, the chief executive officer called a "business meeting." As he entered the CEO's office, Ken learned that *he* was the business under consideration. Present were his wife, his two adult children, his boss, other friends and associates, and the counselor brought in to supervise the intervention.

After Ken got over the initial shock of the surprise gathering, he listened as each of his colleagues, friends, and family members shared how much they cared for him and how they were concerned about his drinking. His response was typical of alcoholics: "I don't believe I have a problem; but if it will make you all feel better, I'll go into the hospital as you wish."

Ken's family had already reserved a bed for him in a thirty-day hospital program, and a few hours later he was admitted. At the hospital, Ken's resistance to facing his illness lessened bit by bit. Not only did he recover, becoming the man we admire and respect today, but he also became a media spokesman for the value of intervention.

*Hospital and residential programs.* Both hospital and residential treatment programs emphasize two categories of medical treatment: physical and psychological. First, there are immediate physical health concerns. An alcoholic or drug addict may require withdrawal or detoxification. There may also be physical damage requiring emergency medical treatment; for example, prolonged bulimia can result in internal bleeding, alcoholism in liver disease. Patients might need nutritional attention, and a variety of internal medicine specialists might be called in as well.

Second, patients in a treatment program need psychiatric evaluation and therapy. Physically removing the patient from the destructive substance or behavior and the environment in which he or she became ill is only a first step, and it may not touch on the cause. Therapy helps the alcoholic discover underlying emotional problems and develop strategies to work through them, so they no longer trigger the destructive responses that caused the disease. At some point close family members may be brought into this therapy. Healthy interpersonal relationships enhance recovery; unhealthy ones perpetuate the problem. Most programs offer support groups for family members and coordinate visits and other interaction with the patient.

In addition to physical treatment and counseling, treatment programs use the group format for education and counseling. Films and speakers explain illness and recovery and teach practical ways to stay healthy, like good nutrition and physical fitness. Many programs require participation in group exercise activities.

Many of the dynamics that lead to chemical dependency or eating disorders are group dynamics. Adult alcoholics typically drink alone, in secret, isolated from others. Teenage addicts often use drugs with others because of peer pressure. Bulimic young women may eat heartily with others, then quickly run to a bathroom to induce vomiting, both the binging and purging the response to how they believe others perceive them. So group therapy and community building are significant aspects of most residential treatment programs. The initial room assignment, who will be roommates, and how many will be in a room are important considerations in some programs. Also, virtually all treatment programs introduce their clients to the Twelve Steps of Alcoholics Anonymous and to support groups as a lifelong strategy to stay well.

In the 1970s Americans were startled when our First Lady announced that, due to dependency on alcohol and prescription drugs, she would enter a residential treatment center. Not only was her recovery and her honesty throughout the process miraculous, the treatment center built around her name and experience has worked miracles in countless lives. The Betty Ford Center in Palm Desert, California, where many of my friends, including clergy, have been treated, is a stellar example of the resources now available to assist recovery from various kinds of addictions.

*Support Groups.* If thousands are helped each year in residential programs, millions enter the road to recovery—and find lifelong support—through peer groups. Most recovering alcoholics, bulimics, and anorexics have found in such groups the key to managing their problems. Those who have initially been turned around through a residential program are normally referred to at least one weekly group activity.

While some may require or prefer groups led by professionals, many addicts have found the miracle of recovery through Alcoholics Anonymous groups or through other groups based on the Twelve Steps of A.A. Narcotics Anonymous groups support those recovering from drug addiction. Overeaters Anonymous meetings serve the needs of those with various eating disorders—anorexia and bulimia as well as overeating. Alanon groups, for spouses of alcoholics, and Alateen, for their children, have also developed from A.A.

How do individuals find their way into such groups? Some began with group meetings as inpatients in hospital-sponsored programs. But most probably were introduced to A.A., N.A., or O.A. by their doctor or clergyperson or a friend suffering the same problems. Groups normally meet once a week in a church hall or some other community meeting room. Some people attend several different meetings a week. Anonymity is protected; first names only are used. The heart of any meeting is personal sharing of how individuals came to hit bottom and how the Twelve Steps are assisting their recovery. Excellent, practical literature is made available. Friendships are formed; more experienced members often provide emergency assistance to those just starting—and to each other—through telephone conversations between meetings. Meetings are open; guests are welcomed. When one meeting gets too large (one A.A. group in Beverly Hills draws hundreds of participants), it divides into more groups.

Most alcoholics and many others afflicted with the difficulties of chemical dependency and eating disorders will be involved in support groups throughout their lives. Alcoholism, for instance, is a disease that one is born with, becoming an active illness whenever the alcoholic drinks. An alcoholic adherent to A.A., even if he has been sober for decades, may say he is recovering from alcoholism but not recovered. He counts on the continued support of A.A. to maintain sobriety. The Twelve Steps of Alcoholics Anonymous have given life and recovery to many suffering people.

## The Twelve-Step Program

In 1939, when it was only four years old, Alcoholics Anonymous first published its Twelve Steps, drawn from religious and medical principles. Briefly presented below, the Twelve Steps are discussed more thoroughly in the book *Twelve Steps and Twelve Traditions.*[3]

*Step One.* "We admitted we were powerless over alcohol—that our lives had become unmanageable." This is bottoming out, the phase of self-honesty when my friend said: "I'm humiliating my kids. I'll stop drinking." Or when the former First Lady admitted, "I am an alcoholic."

*Step Two.* "Came to believe that a Power greater than ourselves could restore us to sanity." Carefully nonsectarian, A.A. teaches that, although the individual alcoholic lacks the resources to turn herself around, religious faith and the help of other alcoholics will support and strengthen her to recover.

*Step Three.* "Made a decision to turn our will and our lives over to the care of God *as we understood Him.*" If the second step is a matter of the mind (belief), the third is a matter of the will, coming to depend on God to point the way to sobriety.

*Step Four.* "Made a searching and fearless inventory of ourselves." The alcoholic describes in writing both her positive qualities and her faults. This begins a process of lifelong self-evaluation. This process enables the alcoholic to overcome fear, pride, and humiliation—emotions which, if unacknowledged, may drive the alcoholic back to the bottle to receive solace.

*Step Five.* "Admitted to God, to ourselves, and to another human being the exact nature of our wrongs." Few alcoholics can stay sober without specifically confessing their misdeeds. The important part is finding the right person in which to confide, and opening up to that person. In addition to sobriety, this process of "coming clean" leads to peace of mind.

*Step Six.* "Were entirely ready to have God remove all these defects of character." In this step the alcoholic must be ready and willing to give up negative personality traits that nonetheless may have been pleasurable.

*Step Seven.* "Humbly asked Him to remove all our shortcomings." A.A. stresses humility as a prerequisite for sobriety. God becomes not a pinch hitter to help out in a crisis but a constant companion, assisting with alcoholism and every other problem in life.

*Step Eight.* "Made a list of all persons we had harmed, and became willing to make amends to them all." In this step the alcoholic writes out a list of all the people he has harmed, directly or indirectly, through his drinking.

*Step Nine.* "Made direct amends to such people whenever possible, except when to do so would injure them or others." Going to those the alcoholic has harmed takes discernment, courage, and understanding. Those who have been harmed are not necessarily emotionally whole themselves. The encounter can be embarrassing and awesome for both parties, and sometimes the injured person may be skeptical about the apology.

*Step Ten.* "Continued to take personal inventory and, when we were wrong, promptly admitted it." Not only must the alcoholic resolve past wrongs, he must also deal with daily wrongdoings immediately, apologizing and asking forgiveness as conflicts arise. This step prevents the alcoholic from creating another sorrowful past.

*Step Eleven.* "Sought through prayer and meditation to improve our conscious contact with God *as we understood Him*, praying only for knowledge of His will for us and the power to carry that out." A.A. stresses spiritual growth both for guidance and for the secure sense of belonging to a caring and loving God.

*Step Twelve.* "Having had a spiritual awakening as the result of these steps, we tried to carry this message to alcoholics and to practice these principles in all our affairs." Earlier I mentioned the church member who would thank me whenever I asked him to help someone struggling with alcohol. "Thank you," he would say, "for helping me stay sober."

The Twelve Steps work. By 1989 an estimated 1.5 million alcoholic men and women in 134 countries had recovered through the Twelve Steps of Alcoholics Anonymous.

## Caring Responses

As I wrote this chapter on how to care for a loved one who is struggling with an addiction, I remembered how others helped—or hurt—me as I sought to control my own overeating. I think that I can remember every negative comment or reaction from at least twenty-five years back. And my struggles have been minor compared to some of the issues we're considering in this chapter.

You will be better equipped to respond to those who abuse their bodies by knowing more about their illnesses and approaches to recovery. Mindful of the complexities of these issues, please consider the following guidelines:

*Be sensitive about issues of self-image and self-esteem.* In many cases, the cause of substance abuse or eating disorders is self-esteem that never developed or was destroyed. In every case, there is a hurting sense of self that either caused or resulted from the uncontrollable intake of drugs, alcohol, or food. In an addictive cycle, the overeater, for instance, eats in order to ease her pain. The overeating, however, results in more pain, so she eats again—and the cycle begins anew.

I have a friend whom I've known since I was a boy. When we were younger, he and I were both overweight. Today he and I still talk about our self-image as "fat boys." We remember the humiliation of wearing jeans for "husky" boys. Even though we've kept our weight under control for over twenty years (he is especially trim), the painful image of being fat did not drop away with our excess pounds.

The alcoholic who has hit bottom and begun recovery is most vulnerable. If he begins to feel humiliated, he may easily fall back on alcohol to ease his pain, thereby starting the cycle of addiction again. Whatever the state of disease or recovery, be generous with your love and support for the alcoholic if not for the behavior. Praise every positive quality and action, especially when he begins to do something about the problem.

**Relate your concern, but don't nag.** My father was a heavy smoker, and my whole family wanted him to quit. Once my brother even put up a poster of a cemetery with the headline "Marlboro Country" over Dad's closet door! But all the nagging we did about his smoking never helped. A smoker since his early teenage years, nicotine had been a part of his entire adult life. Whenever he was under stress, he'd reach for a cigarette. Our nagging became part of that stress! Eventually, in his retirement, he stopped smoking.

When someone close to us seems to have a problem with alcohol, drugs, or food, it may be appropriate to express concern, even if the message is rejected. At this point you are simply planting seeds of awareness that someday may grow large enough to move him to do something about the problem. As I learned with my father's smoking, however, continuous nagging probably won't help. In fact, it may even trigger the compulsive behavior that the individual uses to ease pressure and pain.

*Support and affirm success.* Your wife cuts back to half the number of cigarettes she smoked in the past. Your daughter begins to talk with you about feelings of inadequacy that caused her to starve herself. Your colleague at work orders a soft drink at the company Christmas party and confides that he is joining Alcoholics Anonymous. A close family friend tells you he has lost eighteen pounds in a medical diet program. These are precious moments of celebrating accomplishment, and our response should be positive and complimentary.

You may be invited to attend a meeting of A.A. or another Twelve Step program when your loved one is being recognized for a particular milestone (such as an anniversary of sobriety). Do attend. You'll not only show your loving support, you'll be inspired and strengthened yourself. Remember the self-esteem issue; the recovering person may not realize how far he or she has come without your positive reinforcement.

*Be patient with mistakes and "falling back."* Most recovery programs anticipate temptations and actual falls. A.A. and its family support groups, Alanon and Alateen, deal with the issue of the alcoholic who "slips." Panic is not helpful for anyone involved; neither is guilt or recrimination. Love, support, and encouragement, on the other hand, may help a recovering person pick up from where she left off before her error.

**Consider special circumstances that call for action.** One day there was a terrible automobile accident. A man dressed in a business suit came to the scene of the accident, stopped his car, and jumped out. Going to one of the victims, he talked with her quietly and calmly. Then, suddenly, a woman broke through the crowd of onlookers. She pushed aside the man, shouted, "I'm trained in first aid!" and began to examine the victim from head to toe. The quiet man in the business suit gently spoke into her ear: "Let me know when you are done, Madam. I'm a doctor."

Obviously there are situations in which you are not the appropriate person to take charge. But there may well be times when you are confronted with the problem at a critical moment. When a drunken friend plans to drive himself home or your bulimic teenage baby-sitter begins to cough up blood, you cannot stand idly by, philosophizing about the bottoming out that's soon to occur.

If you are involved in a Twelve Step program, as a part of Step 12 you will be involved in helping others with similar problems. At times you may need guidance from a counselor or other experienced person. Although you will be an invaluable help to other addicts, you shouldn't hesitate to ask for outside help if you are over your head.

*Be supportive of family members of addicts.* Many times you can do little for persons with serious drinking, drug, or eating problems. But you may be of real help to their family members. For years I could do nothing for the bank executive I wrote about at the beginning of this chapter. But I did support her children during the long years when neither they nor I could convince their mother of her problem.

Countless support groups assist loved ones whose lives are disrupted by these problems. Often family members of alcoholics are codependent. Codependent people have low self-esteem and are overly vulnerable to the evaluation of others; the condition can afflict the child of an alcoholic or drug abuser decades after leaving home. There are numerous resources and books on this problem, the most popular being *Codependent No More* by Melodie Beattie.

One of the most memorable lectures I heard while in seminary focused on God's grace. The sophisticated professor who taught theology held the highest credentials, and even the prayers with which he opened his lectures were literary gems. But I'll never forget how he ended his lecture on grace. Himself the recipient of some life-changing and life-saving experiences, he concluded: "The grace of God is not the church's alone to dispense. I know of no organization in history that has served as an agent of divine grace in the lives of people more than Alcoholics Anonymous."[4]

I am blessed to have among my closest friends and

associates many who are victorious, day by day, over chemical abuse and eating disorders. Each of us has problems that limit our living to the fullest. Many of us never deal with our handicaps. But those who do exhibit courage and integrity that inspire and instruct all who know them. I hope your life is blessed with such inspiring relationships.

## ── 15 ──

# When You Are Over
# Your Head

*E*very summer my wife and I take our sons to the same beach. Over the last eight years, we have watched them grow in their water safety skills. They began in a shallow, protected, artificial lagoon, called "the Baby Beach" by the locals. Over time, they graduated to the center of the beach, riding small waves and swimming in water over their heads. Finally, they became confident and competent enough to try the waves at the body-surfing beach, where waves break over your head and can send you somersaulting underwater.

Handling the waves breaking over your head is a key survival skill in other aspects of life, too, including caring for others. When we try to rescue those overwhelmed by waves of crisis or loss, we may find ourselves floundering in the stormy sea with them.

At the body-surfing beach, people watch out for each other. Parents stand where they can guide or rescue a struggling child. Farther out, the expert surfers look out for their peers, and also for the rest of us. If anyone gets too far offshore or becomes overly tired or cuts a foot on the coral reef, one of several friendly hands reaches out to help. The expert surfers, who know the beach and its dangers best, provide the final line of defense.

When the waves of crisis are breaking over your head, you need expert help. In the first four of the scenarios discussed below, you would need to find expert help for your loved one in crisis. In the fifth scenario, you may not need expert help, but you would need tips on how to maintain your own stability when you get exhausted from dealing with difficult people and situations.

### Depression

Everyone gets the blues now and then and may feel down for a time. A favorite person or activity or even a good night's rest can usually cheer us up. But true depression, clinical depression, is like a deep, dark pit from which there is no escape. Even routine challenges of daily living seem overwhelming to the depressed person; she cannot even begin to see creative options and alternatives for solving problems.

True depression is not touched by the loving care of family members and friends. In fact, one way caring persons detect another's depression is when their friend does not respond to their loving support. For example, effective listening meets a need of most persons in crisis, and they open up and talk to a trusted loved one. The depressed person, however, talks very little, except perhaps to make an angry or cynical comment or to give a hollow, distant "yes" or "no."

The first time I attempted to reach out to a deeply depressed person was during my hospital chaplaincy training. A teenage girl with deep psychological problems as well as a life-threatening disease sat and stared at me while I visited and talked; her only words were "hello" when I arrived in her room and "good-bye" when I left. She was empty of signs of emotional life. From that experience and subsequent guidance from my supervisor, I learned about my limitations when someone is severely depressed. Certainly, someone as ill as that young woman requires treatment by a psychiatrist and other doctors in a hospital. My role as a pastor or friend was important but supplemental: indicating my love and concern by visiting; making simple, undemanding small talk; and asking friendly questions requiring a simple "yes" or "no" response.

Depression, like any illness, varies in degrees of severity. Not every clinically depressed person is as seriously ill as my teenage patient or requires hospitalization.

Some depression is heavily veiled. A family member or friend may give the appearance that all is well, carry on seemingly normal conversation, even continue to meet the demands of his or her job. But, as any actor will tell you, such performances when you are not feeling well are demanding, and the strain will begin to show. Symptoms of depression include tiredness from a lack of sleep, excessive sleep, uncharacteristic indecisiveness about even routine matters, lack of appetite, withdrawal from family and friends and favorite activities, or suicidal behavior.

Some depressed persons suffer from manic-depressive (or "bi-polar") disease, characterized by dramatic swings from emotional highs (manic phase) to lows (depressive phase). Modern drug therapy works virtual miracles with many manic-depressive persons.

If depressed behavior persists in a loved one, with the help of other close family members get the depressed person to the professional help he needs. You might begin by taking your loved one to his personal physician. His doctor can eliminate physical causes and direct the depressed person to further psychiatric help, if necessary.

As in the case of anyone undergoing psychiatric therapy, stay in touch and visit as often as possible. As he or she gets well, your support will be most important.

## Suicidal Cues

If you think that a loved one is considering suicide, you are in part responsible for his life or death. You need help in bearing that burden. Even more, the person who is desperate enough to consider suicide as a solution to his problems requires emergency care.

To help a suicidal person, someone must address his underlying problems as well as his impulse to end his life. Few of us have the expertise to deal with such a critical complex of emotional issues.

Of course, by calling in others to help, you risk being the brunt of the anger of the person you care about. But that risk is nothing compared to the risk of your loved one killing himself.

We are facing a national epidemic of teenage suicide, and as a school chaplain who deals with suicidal adolescents, I have felt the pain and anguish of this issue personally. I remember in particular two bright, attractive young men. The first was an honor student and fraternity president in a prominent eastern university. I had known him as his pastor and friend for twelve years. One weekend, he violently took his own life—only a few months after a previous suicide attempt. The second, a depressed high school student who was brought to me by his concerned friends, will probably never forgive me for telling his parents about his plan to kill himself. But today, thank God, he is still alive.

If you find out that a friend is planning to commit suicide, you may struggle with two issues: the nature of confidentiality and whether bringing in next of kin or mental health professionals will somehow push your friend over the edge.

Experts agree that it is crucial to report any suicidal intentions to people who can help—even if that means going against the wishes of the suicidal person, who has begged you to keep his plans confidential. If you struggle with confidentiality, remember that there is a difference between confidentiality and keeping secrets. When an individual shares something confidentially, he or she places confidence in the listener to do what is best for him. In the case of suicidal wishes, doing what's best means not keeping quiet, but telling someone who can help.

What about the risk that bringing in outside help will upset your friend even more? Unfortunately, the risks are greater that your friend or relative *will follow through* on suicide plans if you *don't* get him or her to help.

What are the signs of a suicidal person? When your friend or loved one directly states a plan to commit suicide, take the message seriously. The more specific the person is about a plan, the more literally you should take his words.

Some signs may be more subtle. A suicidal person often puts personal affairs in order, tidying up business matters and making peace in significant relationships. A person who has previously attempted suicide is often likely to try again, especially when under a great deal of stress.

Where should you turn for help? Most communities run suicide prevention hot lines. You may find the number in your telephone directory or by calling the operator or information. Often these hot lines are staffed by well-trained volunteers (who may have come through a suicidal period themselves) with professional counselors on call. They can assist you in responding to your suicidal friend, or they can assist the friend herself.

You can also find help through a trusted family physician or clergyperson. If your suicidal family member or friend has experienced such a crisis before, he or she may know a counselor, clinic, or hospital that helped previously. Ask if you can telephone for an immediate appointment and accompany your troubled loved one to it.

Work in concert with those closest to the suicidal person. If the person is a minor, the policy of most schools and agencies that work with young people is to get the parents involved immediately and assist them in following up with professional attention.

You cannot remove all the risks from a potential suicide crisis. You are dealing with the tangled emotions of another human being over whom you have limited control. But with the right treatment and strong support from loved ones, your relative or friend can not only recover from the crisis but can be emotionally stronger because of it if underlying (and often lifelong) problems are also successfully treated. You may well save a human life!

### Hysteria, Disorientation, and Other Mental Health Crises

A retired friend of mine arrived home one afternoon to find various spills around the house and his normally practical and busy wife feeling weak and dizzy. The whole scene was so uncharacteristic and he was so confounded by it that he got his wife into the car and to the nearest hospital emergency room immediately. Within hours she underwent a major, delicate brain operation from which she required four months to recover. The neurosurgeons said that if my friend had waited another day to get his wife the proper medical treatment, she would have died.

When you encounter uncharacteristic, inappropriate emotional responses from someone you care about, get him or her to a mental health professional or facility for proper treatment. Just as my friend could do nothing about his wife's brain disorder, neither can you deal with uncontrolled hysterical crying and screaming, disorientation about self-identity or location or activity, or other mental problems that pose a threat to the ill person or others. In these cases, you are over your head, and you should get professional help as soon as possible.

## Ethical or Legal Dilemmas

- Your father, while confiding in you that he has prostate cancer, asks you not to tell your mother.

- Your sickly and elderly next-door neighbor confides that her terminally ill husband has worked out a method of suicide with the help of a nurse.

- Your best friend, an airline pilot who has been recently widowed, in an emotional outburst confesses that he is addicted to cocaine.

In moral philosophy, a *dilemma* or *moral problem* is a conflict between two duties or principles or values. In situations like the three summarized above, you may be very clear about what you would do, or you may find yourself floundering indecisively. In matters of ethics, however, not to make a decision *is* a decision.

In making a decision about a dilemma, you can take several approaches. You may look at such dilemmas in terms of what constitutes the most loving and caring course of action (or inaction) for all involved. You may apply the Golden Rule and ask how it would be if you were each of the parties in the ethical conflict. You may consult Scripture, your church's teachings, and your own moral code. And you may compare the values that seem to be conflicting. For example, in the cases above the values that are opposed include: keeping trust with your father versus your mother's right to know his condition; the privacy and dignity of your neighbors versus laws protecting human life; confidentiality and friendship with the pilot versus his health, the law, and the safety of his passengers.

Finally, you might talk out such ethical or legal conflicts with someone you trust. I am blessed with close, perceptive friends who are brutally honest with me when I ask for their true reactions to dilemmas I face. Two are lawyers: one a prosecutor, the other in business law. One is a management consultant; another a high school teacher and counselor. Clergy colleagues (a rabbi, a Presbyterian pastor, and a Roman Catholic priest in addition to my peers in the Episcopal Church) and my wife have given me splendid advice. When I had to decide whether and how to inform some parents that their son was threatening suicide, I talked it over with a few of these friends, who confirmed that I should go to the parents. When I thought about leaving my parish charge of fifteen years to become a school chaplain, I consulted virtually everyone listed above.

I'm sure that you have your own network of caring, competent persons whose advice you can seek when you find yourself caught in an ethical or legal dilemma. If not, you can find resources through churches, counselors, hospitals, and community organizations.

## Difficult Persons and Relationships

What do you do when you can't get along with people you are supposed to love? When every encounter with your mother leaves you feeling depleted and manipulated and small? When your grandfather never fails to end a visit with disapproving comments and a reminder of how you've let the family down? When you can no longer exchange kind words with the mentor and hero of your adult life? When you can't stand even being in the same room with your brother or sister?

Some of my most poignant and heartrending counseling work has centered on how to be caring and attentive toward someone whom an individual loves but doesn't like. These relationships produce frustration, guilt, and emotional exhaustion. Many people seek psychotherapy to resolve such negative feelings toward loved ones. Many simply avoid being involved at all in such difficult relationships.

You may find yourself caring for difficult persons not because you are related to them but through the accidents of circumstance. The obnoxious secretary at the next desk is going through a divorce. The teenage son of the dysfunctional family across the hall in your apartment building has overdosed on drugs. Your roommate in college or in boot camp is struggling to kick dependency on drugs and alcohol.

You may usually get to pick and choose whom you will care for. Sometimes, however, largely because of your own noble qualities and commitment to care, you may feel over your head caring for a very difficult human being. You may find yourself caring for someone who has wrung every other person in his life dry and has begun to wring you dry. You may be trying to care because no one else will.

How should you approach caring for the difficult person? What should you do about your conflicting inclinations and feelings?

*Accept.* If your father has borne you a grudge for thirty years for marrying a divorced man, don't expect a major turnaround as he gets older and more crotchety about life in general. For many difficult persons, the issues that divide you become an obsession. A first step toward caring for persons you don't enjoy being with is to accept them as they are. Don't think you can meet all their needs. Don't try to change into the person they might want you to be or expect them to fulfill your fantasies of how they should be. Accept the limited effect your caring may have on your trying relationship. Don't make your caring contingent on appreciation or an improved relationship. Care because you believe in your heart that it's the right thing to do, and get your satisfaction from knowing in your heart that you did well.

*Commit.* If you are still inclined to care for a person after you accept the realities of the situation, commit yourself to it, at least for a time. Friends of mine, estranged since childhood from the father who abandoned them and their mother during the Depression, committed themselves to stand by him in the weeks before he died. There was simply no one else who would do it. Caring for him brought these daughters a kind of peace and helped them to resolve the bitter grief they had harbored all their lives.

I am often asked to care for persons I find difficult. In those cases I determine to attend to them lovingly no matter what they may say or do, even if no other person on earth can stand to be with them. Love leads to commitment. That's one reason we are able to stick it out with difficult persons.

*Structure.* Realistically, it's one thing to make your commitment, another to live it out. Structure and schedule time to care for those it's easier to avoid. The structure allows you the opportunity to communicate with your troubled friend or family member when you are strongest and least vulnerable to being hurt. It also prevents you from procrastinating and backing down on your commitment. You may find it helpful to explain the boundaries and realities of what you can do. Depending on the relationship and the situation, you may promise to telephone someone daily, or explain that you can make a visit only once a year.

For instance, one of my colleagues was returning to her hometown for a visit. One of her duties included visiting an aunt with whom she'd had a difficult relationship. I suggested she go see her aunt the first morning after she arrived. She would thereby (1) honor her aunt by seeing her first, (2) eliminate early on the emotional burden of anticipating the visit, (3) control the time and setting of the encounter, and (4) fulfill her commitment to perform as a loving niece as best she could.

*Initiate.* Peter, a former parishioner, came to see me regarding his widowed, possessive, demanding mother. Through the years, events had driven them apart. His mother—much to his frustration—contin-ued to treat him as a little boy. Peter loved her and wanted to be a caring son, but she drove him to distraction. He found it increasingly difficult to visit by telephone or in person, so he didn't. She would call, late at night or when he was about to begin a business meeting, and lay guilt on him for being such an uncaring slob; so he avoided contacting her even more, which resulted in her layering more guilt, and so on.

In our discussion, I took Peter through the process: be realistic about expectations, make a real commitment, structure regular contacts with your mother when you can best relate to her, and actively initiate those contacts. We determined together that it would be best if he could be in communication with her once a day, even if only briefly, by telephoning her. By initiating contact, he was able to take control of many aspects of their relationship that had been previously unbearable. Our plan worked and removed much of the conflict and heartache from their relationship.

**Do.** Perform the actions of caring and the gestures of support as best you can within your limitations of time and energy. You may have to evaluate your own performance, because the difficult loved one is not likely to give you affirming feedback. Difficult people do not say, "Enough—I know your husband and children need you at home." Difficult people don't care about your needs. Nor are they grateful. Instead of saying, "Thank you for reroofing the house," they might say, "Now, when are you going to fix the leaky garage?" Do what you can to express your caring by your own reasonable standards, and commend yourself for being a loyal and loving friend or family member.

**Release.** You are a remarkable person, a child of God, gifted with love and caring in your heart. You will be of immeasurable assistance to others in times of crisis. You will do more for them than you could ever know. But you are a finite creature. You lack the power to control circumstances, dictate emotional responses, eliminate losses, remove crises. You are a vulnerable human being who needs the support of others when you face crisis and loss in your own life. You are not here to fulfill anyone else's fantasy of who you should be or what you should do. Neither are others here to fulfill your fantasies. Rather, it is the caring actions themselves that fulfill you and fill you with joy and peace.

Caring for someone else should not make you sick! You can't care for anyone when you're sick. Just as effective parents learn to release their children at the appropriate time, so effective care givers learn to release those they would help after giving all they can. Releasing someone to the care of God is a spiritual act. It is an act of trust, of faith, hope, and love.

Caring for people in crisis situations is difficult, draining work. But remember: your every act of caring, your every attempt at caring, helps restore faith, hope, and love to our planet. Hang in there.

# Appendix

Listed below are organizations pertaining to the major kinds of crisis and loss situations covered in this book. The final listing tells you how to reach a clearinghouse that will direct you to groups concerned with other kinds of problems.

## Resources and Organizations

### AGING

American Association of Retired Persons
(AARP)
601 E Street NW
Washington, D.C. 20049
(202) 434-2277
(800) 424-3410

National Institute on Aging Information Center
P.O. Box 8057
Gaithersburg, MD 20890
(800) 222-2225

### AIDS

The Foundation for Children with AIDS
1800 Columbus Avenue
Boston, MA 02119
(617) 442-7442

National AIDS Information Clearinghouse
P.O. Box 6003
Rockville, MD 20849-6003
(800) 458-5231

National HIV and AIDS Hot Line
(800) 342-AIDS
In Spanish, (800) 344-7432
Deaf access, (800) AIDS-TTY (243-7889)

## ALCOHOLISM

Alcoholics Anonymous (A.A.)
P.O. Box 459
Grand Central Station
New York, NY 10163
(212) 870-3400

Al-Anon Family Groups
P.O. Box 862
Midtown Station
New York, NY 10018-0862
(212) 302-7240
(800) 245-4656

National Council on Alcoholism and Drug
Dependence
12 West 21st Street
New York, NY 10010
(212) 206-6770
(800) NCA-CALL

# ALZHEIMER'S DISEASE

Alzheimer's Association
919 North Michigan Avenue, Suite 1000
Chicago, IL 60611
(312) 335-8700
(800) 621-0379

Alzheimer's Disease Education and Referral
Center
P.O. Box 8250
Silver Spring, MD 20907-8250
(800) 438-4380

# ARTHRITIS

Arthritis Foundation
1314 Spring St. NW
Atlanta, GA 30309
(404) 872-7100
(800) 283-7800

# AUTISM

Autism Society of America
7910 Woodmont Avenue, Suite 650
Bethesda, MD 20814
(301) 657-0881

# BLINDNESS

National Federation of the Blind
1800 Johnson Street
Baltimore, MD 21230
(410) 659-9314

## CANCER

American Cancer Society
1599 Clifton Road NE
Atlanta, GA 30329
(404) 320-3333
(800) ACS-2345

Candlelighters Childhood Cancer Foundation
7910 Woodmont Avenue, Suite 460
Bethesda, MD 20814
(301) 657-8401
(800) 366-2223

National Alliance of Breast Cancer
Organizations
1180 Avenue of the Americas, 2nd Floor
New York, NY 10036
(212) 719-0154

## CEREBRAL PALSY

United Cerebral Palsy Associations
1522 K Street NW
Suite 1112
Washington, D.C. 20005
(202) 842-1266
(800) 872-5827

## CHILD ABUSE

CHILDHELP, U.S.A.
6463 Independence Ave.
Woodland Hills, CA 91367
(818) 347-7280
(800) 4-A-CHILD

Parents Anonymous
520 S. Lafayette Park Place, Suite 316
Los Angeles, CA 90057
(213) 388-6685
(800) 421-0353

## CYSTIC FIBROSIS

Cystic Fibrosis Foundation
6931 Arlington Road
Bethesda, MD 20814
(301) 951-4422
(800) FIGHT-CF

## DEATH OF A CHILD

The American Sudden Infant Death Syndrome
Institute
6065 Roswell Road, Suite 876
Atlanta, GA 30328
(404) 843-1030
(800) 232-SIDS
In Georgia, (800) 847-SIDS

The Compassionate Friends
P.O. Box 3696
Oak Brook, IL 60522
(708) 990-0010

SIDS (Sudden Infant Death Syndrome)
Alliance
10500 Little Patuxent Parkway, Suite 420
Columbia, MD 21044
(800) 221-SIDS

## DIABETES

American Diabetes Association
National Center
1660 Duke St.
Alexandria, VA 22314
(703) 549-1500
(800) 232-3472

Juvenile Diabetes Foundation International
432 Park Avenue South
New York, NY 10016
(212) 889-7575
(800) JDF-CURE

## DOWN SYNDROME

National Down Syndrome Congress
1605 Chantilly Drive, Suite 250
Atlanta, GA 30324
(404) 633-1555
(800) 232-NDSC

National Down Syndrome Society
666 Broadway
New York, NY 10012
(212) 460-9330
(800) 221-4602

## DRUG ABUSE

Narcotics Anonymous
P.O. Box 9999
Van Nuys, CA 91406
(818) 780-3951

Nar-Anon Family Groups
P.O. Box 2562
Palos Verdes Peninsula, CA 90274
(310) 547-5800

National Clearinghouse for Alcohol and Drug
Information
P.O. Box 2345
Rockville, MD 20847
(301) 468-2600
(800) 729-6686 (1-800-SAY-NO-TO)

## EATING DISORDERS

American Anorexia/Bulimia Association
418 East 76th Street
New York, NY 10021
(212) 734-1114

National Association of Anorexia Nervosa and
Associated Disorders (A.N.A.D.)
P.O. Box 7
Highland Park, IL 60035
(708) 831-3438

Overeaters Anonymous
World Service Office
P.O. Box 92870
Los Angeles, CA 90009
(310) 618-8835

## EMOTIONAL PROBLEMS

Emotions Anonymous
P.O. Box 4245
St. Paul, MN 55104-0245
(612) 647-9712

## EPILEPSY

The Epilepsy Foundation of America
4351 Garden City Drive
Landover, MD 20785
(301) 459-3700
(800) 332-1000
National Epilepsy Library
(800) EFA-4050

## GAMBLING

Gamblers Anonymous
P.O. Box 17173
Los Angeles, CA 90017
(213) 386-8789

## GENETIC DISORDERS

Alliance of Genetics Support Groups
38th and R Streets NW
Washington, D.C. 20057
(800) 336-4363

National Organization for Rare Disorders
P.O. Box 8923
New Fairfield, CT 06812
(203) 746-6518

## HEART DISEASE

American Heart Association
7272 Greenville Avenue
Dallas, TX 75231
(214) 373-6300
(800) 242-8721

The Mended Hearts, Inc.
7272 Greenville Avenue
Dallas, TX 75231-4596
(214) 706-1244

## HOSPICE CARE

Children's Hospice International
901 North Washington Street, Suite 700
Alexandria, VA 22314
(703) 684-0330
(800) 242-4453

Hospice Education Institute
Hospicelink
190 Westbrook Road
Essex, CT 06426
(203) 767-1620
(800) 331-1620

## HUNTINGTON'S DISEASE

Huntington's Disease Society of America
140 W. 22nd St.
New York, NY 10011
(212) 242-1968
(800) 345-HDSA

# LEARNING DISABILITIES

Learning Disabilities Association of America
4156 Library Road
Pittsburgh, PA 15234
(412) 341-8077
(412) 341-1515

The Orton Dyslexia Society
P.O. Box 9888
Baltimore, MD 21284
(410) 296-0232
(800) 222-3123

# LUNG DISEASE

American Lung Association
1740 Broadway
New York, NY 10019
(212) 315-8700

# MENTAL RETARDATION

The Arc
500 East Border Street, Suite 300
Arlington, TX 76010
(817) 261-6003

# MULTIPLE SCLEROSIS

National Multiple Sclerosis Society
733 Third Avenue
New York, NY 10017
(212) 986-3240
(800) 532-7667

# MUSCULAR DYSTROPHY

Muscular Dystrophy Association
3300 East Sunrise Drive
Tuscon, AZ 85718
(602) 529-2000
(800) 572-1717

# PARALYSIS

American Paralysis Association
500 Morris Avenue
Springfield, NJ 07081
(201) 379-2690
(800) 225-0292
Spinal Cord Injury Hot Line
(800) 526-3456

National Spinal Cord Injury Association
600 West Cummings Park, Suite 2000
Woburn, MA 01801
(617) 935-2722
(800) 962-9629

# PARKINSON'S DISEASE

Parkinson's Educational Program
3900 Birch Street, Suite 105
Newport Beach, CA 92660
(714) 250-2975
(800) 344-7872

## RUNAWAYS

Runaway Hot Line
P.O. Box l2428
Austin, TX 78711
(800) 231-6946
In Texas, (800) 392-3352

## SICKLE CELL DISEASE

National Association for Sickle Cell Disease
3345 Wilshire Boulevard, Suite 1106
Los Angeles, CA 90010
(213) 736-5455
(800) 421-8453

## SINGLE PARENTS

Parents Without Partners
8807 Colesville Road
Silver Spring, MD 20910
(301) 588-9355
(800) 637-7974

## TEENAGE BEHAVIORAL PROBLEMS

Families Anonymous
P.O. Box 3475
Culver City, CA 90231-3475
(310) 313-5800
(800) 736-9805

## WIDOWED PERSONS

Widowed Persons Service
American Association of Retired Persons
601 E Street NW
Washington, D.C. 20049
(202) 434-2277

## REFERRALS FOR OTHER PROBLEMS

National Center for Health Information
P.O. Box 1133
Washington, D.C. 20013-1133
(800) 336-4797

# Endnotes

*Introduction*

1. From a sermon by the Reverend Norman Ishizaki of Los Angeles.

*Chapter 1: Be Aware of Your Own Feelings*

1. Paul Tournier, *The Meaning of Persons* (San Francisco: Harper & Row, 1982), 153–58.
2. Elisabeth Kubler-Ross, *On Death and Dying* (New York: Collier Books, 1970), 38–49.
3. This metaphor was taught to my wife and me in a parent group led by Dr. Susan Brown of Los Angeles.
4. Tournier, *The Meaning of Persons*, 123–34.

*Chapter 2: Act*

1. John Bradshaw, *Coming Home*. PBS series, available on videotape.

*Chapter 3: Be*

1. From a sermon by the Reverend Janey Smith of Los Angeles.
2. John Naisbitt, *Megatrends* (New York: Warner Books, 1982), 39–53.

3. I am indebted to my seminary pastoral counseling professor, Dr. John Romig Johnson, now in private practice in New York City, for many of these descriptive phrases.
4. Tournier, *The Meaning of Persons.*

Chapter 5: Understand the Emotions of Grief
1. Kubler-Ross, *On Death and Dying,* 38–49.
2. Viktor E. Frankl, *Man's Search for Meaning* (New York: Washington Square Press, 1984), Part I.
3. Kubler-Ross, *On Death and Dying,* 112–57.

Chapter 6: Know Available Resources
1. Alan Loy McGinnis, *The Friendship Factor* (Minneapolis: Augsburg Publishing House, 1979).
2. Kubler-Ross, *On Death and Dying.*
3. Alcoholics Anonymous, *Twelve Steps and Twelve Traditions* (New York: Alcoholics Anonymous World Services, 1989). The Twelve Steps of A.A. are reprinted with permission of Alcoholics Anonymous World Services, Inc.
4. For instance, Leo Buscaglia, *Living, Loving and Learning* (Thorofare, N.J.: Charles B. Slack, Inc., 1982).

Chapter 9: With the Terminally Ill
1. Kubler-Ross, *On Death and Dying,* 38–137.

Chapter 14: When Dealing with Chemical Dependency and Eating Disorders
1. Alcoholics Anonymous, *Twelve Steps,* 77.
2. Alcoholics Anonymous, *Twelve Steps,* 2.
3. Alcoholics Anonymous, *Twelve Steps,* 21–125.
4. Quote from the Reverend Doctor James A. Carpenter of the General Theological Seminary, New York City.

The author requests your comments, reactions, and suggestions. Perhaps you have a special story of caring in which you helped a friend or relative in a crisis. Or perhaps someone or some organization was especially helpful to you. Please indicate whether your story may be shared with others and whether you prefer anonymity or will allow your name to be used.

Please write:

The Reverend M. Gregory Richards
P.O. Box 16414
Beverly Hills, CA 90209